Daoist China

Governance

Economics

Culture

Livia Kohn

Three Pines Press
P. O. Box 530416
St. Petersburg, FL 33747
www.threepinespress.com

9 8 7 6 5 4 3 2 1

Printed in the United States of America
This edition is printed on acid-free paper that meets the American National Standard Institute Z39.48 Standard.
Distributed in the United States by Three Pines Press.

Illustrations:
Photographs by Thomas L. Moscarillo: Preface, 5, 9, 10, 12, 13, 16, 17, 21, 22, 24, 26, 27, 28, 32, 35, 37, 38, 39, 40, 44, 46, 47, 48, 50, 51, 53, 58, 59, 60
Photographs by Helene Minot: 1, 6, 11, 14, 15, 20, 23, 25, 29, 31, 33, 34, 41, 42, 49, 55, 56
Photographs from Public Domain: 2, 3, 4, 7, 11, 18, 19, 30, 43, 45, 52, 54, 57
Photograph by Robin R. Wang: 8; Photograph by Liu Xun, 36

Cover Art: "Airplane over Temple." Photograph by Thomas L. Moscarillo. Cover design by Lea Lagueux.

Library of Congress Cataloging-in-Publication Data

Names: Kohn, Livia, 1956- author.
Title: Daoist China : governance, economics, culture / Livia Kohn.
Description: St. Petersburg, FL : Three Pines Press, 2018. | Includes bibliographical references.
Identifiers: LCCN 2017061723 (print) | LCCN 2018000143 (ebook) | ISBN 9781931483377 | ISBN 9781931483353 (pbk. : alk. paper)
Subjects: LCSH: Taoism--China--History--21st century. | Taoism--Customs and practices. | China--Civilization--2002-
Classification: LCC BL1910 (ebook) | LCC BL1910 .K636 2018 (print) | DDC 299.5/140951--dc23
LC record available at https://lccn.loc.gov/2017061723

Contents

Part One: Governance

Part Two: Economy

Part Three: Culture

Preface

When giving lectures at Beijing Normal University in July 2017, I also went to Xi'an to explore various Daoist and historical sites. Taking the train between the two cities (about 4-5 hours each way) and walking about in the searing heat, I observed continued unbridled construction of huge, megalithic high-rise complexes in vast stretches of the country, complete with the untrammeled despoiling of nature and intensification of pollution, as well as the ever increasing vibrancy of the Chinese people, glued to their cell phones and actively connected online, always moving about and hustling for yet another deal.

At the same time, using the internet without a VPN and talking to colleagues at the university, I was struck by the massive increase in repressive measures by the state, the tightening of the intellectual control in both content and expression, the fluctuating inaccessibility of information sources that used to be perfectly fine. What, I asked myself, is going on here? Where stands China today and where is it headed from here? And what, in all of this, is the role and place of Daoism?

After returning home, I dove into an intensive exploration, reading anything and everything I could lay my hands on regarding the politics, economics, culture, and religion of China today, focusing particularly on works published in the last two years. I have come to see the Chinese situation in a new and rather disturbing light and am now ready to share my observations in the following sixty vignettes.

Part 1

Governance

1. The China Experiment

Since its founding in 1949, the People's Republic of China has been engaged in the most immense and radical social experiment on the planet: the remaking of an entire civilization, culture, and society in the direction of a utopian, socialist, and modern ideal.

It has done so through a series of campaigns and organized structural changes, beginning in the 1950s with the Land Reform that redistributed all privately owned land, taking it away from established landowners, nationalizing it, then handing it over to poor peasants to farm. By the middle of the decade, pushing to eradicate private ownership, wipe out commercial activities, suppress capitalist thought, and turn all citizens into members of the state, the government enforced radical collectivization, where everyone was assigned to a work unit (*danwei* 单位) and, continuing imperial policy, each family had to obtain a local household registration (*hukou* 户口). All property and all activities became communal, to the point where people's houses did no longer have kitchens as everyone ate in collective dining rooms, or spaces for children since all infants were raised in communal creches.

The Great Leap Forward in 1958 enhanced this development through centrally assigned farming directives, combined with a nationwide effort to produce steel from all kinds of metals, including farm implements, in backyard furnaces. The result was a massive crop failure that led to three years of famine, during which nearly 45 million people died.

The death toll increased during the Cultural Revolution, which began in 1966 when Mao Zedong 毛泽东 called upon young people, the Red Guards, to destroy everything old—culture, habits, artifacts, even people. Millions of city dwellers were sent into the countryside to learn from the peasants, while innumerable cultural treasures were defaced or destroyed. It ended with Mao's death in 1976.

The Four Modernizations under Deng Xiaoping 邓小平, starting in 1978 with a focus on agriculture, industry, defense and science, embodied a more modern vision of socialist China. Being rich was no longer frowned upon nor were private initiative or individual differences. Opening China to Western investments, first in several Special Economic Zones on the southeastern seaboard, Deng guided it to become the workshop of the world and a major export power. Instituting the one-child policy in 1980, he engineered new family structures and limited population growth. As a result, the Chinese economy tripled over the next thirty years, and a third of its now 1.3 billion people rose into the middle class.

Socialism with Chinese characteristics, as it has evolved since then—interrupted by a period of four more repressive years after a pro-democracy movement was violently suppressed in June 1989—envisions a modern, industrialized, urbanized society made up of well-educated, healthy, and prosperous people who work and live together in harmony and spread peace and abundance. Hu Jintao 胡锦涛, who led China from 2002-2012, formulated it in terms of Eight Honors and Eight Disgraces:

> Love the country; do it no harm.
> Serve the people; never betray them.
> Follow science; discard ignorance.
> Be diligent; not indolent.
> Be united, help each other;
> Make no gains at others' expense.
> Be honest and trustworthy;
> Do not sacrifice ethics for profit.
> Be disciplined and law-abiding;
> Never be chaotic and lawless.
> Live plainly, work hard;
> Do not wallow in luxuries and pleasures.

His successor, the current leader Xi Jinping 习近平, while working hard to extirpate corruption in government and industry, describes it in terms of the China Dream (*Zhongguo meng* 中国梦), similarly endorsing the ideal of social justice and overarching harmony. This plays out internationally through the One Belt, One Road (*yidai yilu* 一带一路) initiative that supports major infrastructure projects in developing countries, opening them to commerce while enhancing Chinese influence while securing raw materials.

Internally, Xi Jinping's socialism manifests in an enhanced public surveillance network called the Social Credit System (SCS). Currently tested in various cities, it is scheduled to become mandatory nationwide in 2020. It uses digital technology to monitor people's daily activities: where and with whom they live; what they buy in stores and online; where they go and how they get there; how much debt they have; whether they pay their bills on time; who their friends are and how they interact with them; what they watch on TV; what kinds of websites they visit; and so on.

Based on close observation, CSC classifies behavior according to four distinct categories: honesty in government affairs, commercial integrity, social integrity, and judicial credibility. Government-sponsored companies that combine financial and internet know-how are charged with gathering and evaluating all these data. Eventually they will assign a credit rating of up to 1000 points to each and every member of Chinese society, placing each individual in one of four ranks

The envisioned ideal is, as the original directive states, to "forge a public opinion environment where keeping trust is glorious," where people are being shamed into doing the right thing. To do so, all scores are made public, allowing friends, neighbors, and coworkers to know exactly what each one is doing and how trustworthy they are. The ranking, then, combined with public opinion, in effect creates a new caste system.

People with a low rating would find their lives greatly complicated, making interaction with government offices, health care centers, and other agencies slow and laborious. They would not be able to get passports to travel, purchase airline or high-speed train tickets, stay in posh hotels, or purchase real estate. Even worse, their children would be barred from even applying to better-level schools.

People with a high score, on the other hand, would be the new privileged class, getting the red-carpet treatment wherever they go. For example, a score of 600 or more would allow them to take out an easy loan for shopping, rent a car without a deposit, receive faster check-in at hotels, and get VIP treatment at airports and railway stations. Businesses, too, would be subject to the System, a good score based on government approval securing government support, which then translates into lower tax rates, easier credit, and better investment opportunities. Thus, the great China experiment continues, as always led by the Chinese Communist Party.

YouTube: "Mosaic: The China Dream"

"Social Credit Score"

Read: Benson, Linda. 2016. *China since 1949*. London: Routledge.

Pillsbury, Michael. 2015. *The Hundred-Year Marathon: China's Secret Strategy to Replace America as the Global Superpower*. New York: Henry Holt & Co.

2. The Party

The driving force behind the great China experiment is the Chinese Communist Party, founded with Soviet help in 1927 and rising to prominence during the anti-Japanese war, when its members cooperated with the peasants rather than suppressing and exploiting them as the Nationalists did. After the Japanese withdrew in 1945, the Communists gained control in a bloody civil war and founded the People's Republic in 1949.

Closely following the Leninist and Stalinist model, the Party under Mao developed into the centrally ruled, authoritarian organization that it is today, with 85 million members or one in every fifteen citizens. The core of power lies with the Party Secretary, selected among nine members of the Standing Committee of the 25-member Politburo. It in turn sits at the center of a vast and largely secret system, controlling both the military and civil administration through Party committees on all five levels of government—provinces, cities, counties, townships, and villages.

The Party is the legislative arm of the Chinese government, setting policies, making all rules, and creating all laws. The government proper is its executive, also entirely dependent on the Party. The Party staffs all ministries and agencies through an elaborate and opaque appointments system; it instructs them on policy through behind-the-scenes committees; and guides their political posture and public statements through the propaganda network. The officials working in public institutions are trained, and retrained at regular intervals, through the Party's extensive nationwide network of 2,800 schools, now called Civil Management Training Centers, before they are eligible for promotion.

The judiciary branch, too, is firmly in Party hands. All decisions and punishments meted out by the courts occur at the behest and direction of Party organs, which ultimately control the judges directly and the lawyers indirectly through legal associations and licensing.

As well as sitting above state-owned enterprises and regulatory agencies, Party departments oversee key think-tanks, the courts, the media, approved religions, and other organizations as well as all universities and educational institutions. They also exert considerable influence on many private companies. To maintain power, moreover, the Party has eradicated political rivals, eliminated the autonomy of the courts and press, restricted religion and civil society, denigrated rival versions of nationhood, centralized political power, established extensive networks of security police, and dispatched dissidents to labor camps (MacGregor 2010, 15, xxii).

No other central party of a similar nature has survived this long—they were either destroyed through military intervention (as in Germany and Cambodia), collapsed into different forms of authoritarian government (as in Russia) or gave way to democratic institutions (as in Taiwan and the former East Bloc countries). The Chinese Communist Party, too, shows signs of an end-stage Leninist institution. Thus, most leading members have either property or citizenship abroad, ready to jump ship at a moment's notice.

To shore up its power and rally the people's support, the Party today engages in wide publicity campaigns and makes major efforts to curb corruption. As this succeeds and the economy flourishes, more people take pride in being Chinese, and nationalist sentiments grow. Still, protests are numerous, typically centering on real estate, health care, and pollution, and any number of incidents—natural disasters, terrorist acts, economic failure—can potentially set off cataclysmic changes.

Daoists participate in both ends of the spectrum, finding much to improve in the society while also supporting nationalism, especially as they see themselves as the major indigenous organized religion of the country.

YouTube: "Explained: China's Communist Party"

Read: Li, Xiaobing, and Xiansheng Tian. 2017. *Urbanization and Party Survival in China: People vs. Power*. Lanham, MD: Lexington Books.

McGregor, Richard. 2011. *The Party: 1.3 Billion People, 1 Secret Regime*. London: Penguin.

Shambaugh, David. 2016. *China's Future*. Cambridge: Polity Press.

3. Religious Control

Organized religions, with their power to mobilize large numbers of people for potentially rebellious activities, have long been suspect to the Chinese state. Thus, the first ruler of the Ming dynasty, Emperor Taizu (r. 1368–1399), himself catapulted into power by a religious rebellion, decreed a number of administrative measures of control. Most of these remained in place until the founding of the Republic of China in 1912 and serve as ancestors of religious control today.

For example, he made all religious affairs subject to approval and control by the Ministry of Rites. Within this institution, all members and activities were supervised by the Bureau of Daoist / Buddhist Registration, which had branch offices in each province, prefecture, and district. In this way, even the most remote religious activity occurring in the empire could be monitored and controlled by an arm of the central government.

Among other things, the registration offices were responsible for issuing and monitoring ordination certificates, official passports for monks and nuns, which they had to carry at all times. In addition, they were subject to the All-Knowing Register, an official list with the names of all practitioners who had ever spent any time in a monastery.

Only specially designated monasteries were allowed to hold ordinations, ceremonies were limited to once in three, five, or even ten years, and the number of monks and nuns was restricted to serve the government's needs. Private temples, owned and sponsored by local aristocrats, were severely curtailed and had to have an official stamp of approval. The overall effect of these measures was twofold: it reduced enthusiasm for the religious path among the population and it led to a high level of standardization among institutions and practitioners.

The modern equivalent of the Ministry of Rites is the Bureau of Religious Affairs. It acknowledges five religions: Buddhism, Daoism, Islam, Catholicism, and Protestantism—defining religion along Western models rather than indigenous qualities and strictly limiting approved forms. For example, it does not accept the leadership position of the Pope, so that the official Chinese Catholic Church is separate from Rome. Only groups and organizations properly accredited can run places of worship and make use of their land, goods, and income. Whether a Buddhist monastery, Daoist temple, Muslim mosque, or Christian church, all are subject to state regulations—which they have to post in their reception area. Their inhabitants, moreover, are state employees who receive a monthly stipend from the government.

This limitation has resulted in the flourishing of large numbers of so-called underground churches or temples—of all denominations—which are monitored by the Ministry of State Security, aka the secret police, and for the most part left alone, with periodic bouts of harassment. The pervasive presence and much advanced state of internet technology impacts this in several ways. On the one hand, it makes surveillance and control easier for the state; on the other hand, instant messaging and other apps, like the ubiquitous WeChat, allow practitioners to be in constant contact and take evasive action as needed.

The heir of the Bureau of Registration today is the network of religious associations, counseling committees consisting of religious representatives, prominent lay followers, scholars, and local officials. They serve as the administrative link between the Bureau of Religious Affairs and the people on the ground. Just like in the Ming dynasty established in a hierarchical pattern that reaches throughout the entire country, these associations intensify the interference of the government in religious matters. Thus, for example, all Buddhist temples are controlled by the Chinese Buddhist Association with headquarters in the Guangjisi 广济寺 (Temple of Wide Salvation) in Beijing. Advanced practitioners are subject to its guidance as they train at the Buddhist Academy at the Fayuansi 法源寺 (Source of Dharma Temple) of the Chan school and the Yonghegong 雍和宫 (Palace of Peace and Harmony, i.e., Lama Temple) of the Tantric school.

YouTube: "Is China an Atheist Country?"

Read: Yang, Fenggang. 2012. *Religion in China Today: Survival and Revival under Communist Rule*. New York: Oxford University Press, chs. 4-5.

Taylor, Romeyn. 1973. "The Social Origins of the Ming Dynasty, 1351-1360." *Monumenta Serica* 22:1-78.

4. The Chinese Daoist Association

The Chinese Daoist Association (Zhongguo daojiao xiehui 中国道教协会) was founded in 1957 to serve as a forum for interaction with the state. Interrupted in its work during the Cultural Revolution (1966-1976), when all religious activity was outlawed and the clergy had to return to the laity, it has since established branches in each province and district, created systematic registration of all monastics, founded several Daoist academies for advanced training, arranged for formal ordinations, and sponsored major rituals. Its recent leaders, Ren Farong 任法融 (b. 1936) and Li Guangfu 李光富 (b. 1955), have expanded its scope and moved toward wider international outreach.

Its organization, just like the Party, is strictly hierarchical. Beijing at the top has authority over the provincial branches, which in turn head the regional subdivisions in charge of county chapters. One does not have a choice in joining the Daoist Association: all monastics and Daoist masters are members by default as well as some lay councilmen. This was the main condition under which they could reinvest in religious institutions after the Cultural Revolution.

Additional participants include scholars of Daoism and representatives of relevant municipal services. Thus, all the principal actors of religious activity—clerics, and monastics, lay followers, scholars, and local officials—are under close supervision of the state, which watches their every move and to which they are accountable.

In Party-speak, the Chinese Daoist Association is, as Adeline Herrou translates, "patriotic religious organization that assists the government in its honorable and far-seeing religious policies, exhorts religious adepts to love the country and its religion while facilitating research on Daoist culture, harmonizing religious activities, organizing participation, and activating followers to serve the economic and cultural construction of the motherland" (2013, 92).

One way it controls the religion is through land management. Since all land belongs to the state and all religious properties were confiscated after 1949, negotiating the return and rebuilding of temples is often a long, drawn-out process that results in various levels of reconstruction and reorganization. Local committees keep a close eye on the reemerging religious community, always making sure that it remains in line with the framework set by the state.

In addition, the Association controls the appointment of religious leaders. Thus, the abbots, especially of larger monasteries are not elected among the brethren in-house but chosen by a council of monastics as well as state representatives in charge of the Daoist Association.

Another way of control is through publications that standardize terminology and approve schools and practices by listing them in the *Daojiao dacidian* 道教大辞典 (Great Dictionary of the Daoist Religion) first published in 1994, as well as in its official journal, called *Zhongguo daojiao* 中国道教 (Chinese Daoism). In addition, headquarters also publishes books for young monastics that are distributed widely through the temple network. They outline monastic rules and regulations together with approved and accepted ritual practices. A prominent example is Min Zhiting's 闽智亭 (1924-2004) *Daojiao yifan* 道教仪范 (Observances of the Daoist Religion; 1986). All local associations are similarly held to publish not only newsletters of their activities but also accounts of the state of their particular institutions and records of local import.

YouTube: "Proponents of Taoism Want to Bring It into the 21st Century"

Read: Herrou, Adeline. 2013. *A World of Their Own: Monastics and Their Community in Contemporary China*. St. Petersburg, Fla.: Three Pines Press.

5. The White Cloud Temple

The Chinese Daoist Association has its main headquarters at the Baiyun guan 白云观 (White Cloud Temple) in Beijing. Also called the First Temple under Heaven, it was founded in the Tang dynasty and came fully into its own under the Mongols, when Kublai Khan (r. 1260-1294) made Beijing the capital.

His grandfather Genghis Khan (1162-1227) summoned the Daoist leader and alchemist Qiu Chuji 邱处机, aka Changchun 长春 (1148-1227), to his Central Asian capital in 1220 and—despite the fact that Qiu did not have a handy elixir of immortality to offer—made him the chief of *all* religions of China. When Qiu settled in the Baiyun guan as his main residence in the capital, it became the seat of the state's overarching religious administration and has remained in this position ever since.

The temple is located about 2.5 miles west and slightly south of Tian'anmen Square in the city center. Like all religious and palatial edifices, it consists of a series of buildings laid out on a south-to-north axis and divided by various open courtyards. After entering the main gate and crossing a narrow stone bridge said to stop harmful winds, the first building honors the Numinous Officials (Lingguan 灵官), the guardian deities of the religion. Next, flanked by bell and drum towers, comes the sanctuary to the Jade Emperor (Yuhuang 玉皇), the head of the celestial administration.

Beyond this are three increasingly sacred halls, honoring Daoist commandments (*laolü* 老律), the patriarch Qiu Chuji, and the Three Pure Ones (Sanqing 三清), the gods of the three central Daoist heavens and their scriptures. They include the creator god Heavenly Worthy of Primordial Beginning (Yuanshi tianzun 元始天尊), the revelatory deity God of the Dao (Daojun 道君), and the hands-on savior Highest Lord Lao (Taishang Laojun 太上老君). At the very back is an ordination platform, where novices receive precepts and scriptures. There are lovely murals and stone steles, including the original version of the famous *Neijing tu* 内经图 (Chart of Internal Passageways), a key document of internal alchemy (see #57 below).

While this makes up the central axis of the monastery, the torso of its body, its sides constitute the extremities. Traditionally that would be where residential and administrative quarters were located, together with bath houses, kitchen, and dining facilities. These are today in a side compound, not accessible to the public.

Instead the sides of the main body house further deities, including on the west the popular group of the good-fortune bringing Eight Immortals (*baxian* 八仙), their chief and master Lü Dongbin 吕洞宾, as well as the influential abbot Wang Kunyang 王崑陽, aka Changyue 长月 (1622-1680), who codified the priestly ranks and precepts in the early Qing dynasty.

On the east, moreover, we find a shrine dedicated to Hua Tuo 华佗 (d. 208), an early master of Chinese medicine best known as the creator of the popular qigong form Five Animals Frolic, together with several more elemental deities. They include thunder gods, the deity of fire, and the Perfect Warrior (Zhenwu 真武), the well-worshiped protector of the north and the state.

YouTube: "White Clouds Temple"

Read: Waley, Arthur. 1931. *The Travels of an Alchemist*. London: George Routledge & Sons.

Yoshioka, Yoshitoyo. 1979. "Taoist Monastic Life." In *Facets of Taoism*, edited by Holmes Welch and Anna Seidel, 220-52. New Haven, Conn.: Yale University Press.

6. Complete Perfection

The Daoist school that runs the Baiyun guan and by extension all of Daoism in China is called Complete Perfection or Complete Reality (Quanzhen 全真). It goes back to the 12th century and was founded by Wang Chongyang 王重阳 (1112–1170), the son of local gentry in northwest China (Shaanxi).

After receiving a classical education, he spent most of his life as an official in the military administration of the Central Asian dynasty of the Jurchen-Jin (1125-1260). In 1159, at age forty-eight, Wang retired from office and withdrew to the Zhongnan mountains 钟南山 near modern Xi'an, where he built a thatched hut and began to lead the life of an eccentric hermit. After a revelatory experience, during which Lü Dongbin appeared to him, he intensified his practice even more. In 1167, he burned his hut to the ground and moved to Shandong in eastern China, where he preached his visions and founded various religious communities until his death in 1170.

His work was continued by seven disciples, six men and one woman, known collectively as the Seven Perfected (*qizhen* 七真). Late immortalized in popular fiction, they observed the standard three-year mourning period for their master, then went their separate ways to spread his teaching, each founding communities and developing separate lineages (*pai* 派). Qiu Chuji was one of them, the founder of the leading Longmen 龙门 (Dragon Gate) lineage, still in charge today.

Complete Perfection is fundamentally an ascetic school. Adepts are vegetarian and celibate, residing in monastic communities that follow the administrative model of Chan (Zen) Buddhism, the dominant religious organization in Song China. Also spending time in solitary seclusion, retreats lasting up to 100 days, they observe stringent precepts and community rules along with Confucian-based ethics—a feature that endears the school to ruling powers. Encouraged to study with more than one master, they also undergo a period of "wandering like the clouds," where they become mendicants for several years, spending much time on the road and temporarily joining various communities.

Their practice, besides performing morning and evening services, during which they chant sacred scriptures and spells, focuses on internal alchemy, the systematic inner refinement of personal into cosmic energy, that is, transmuting vital (sexual) essence first into life energy (*qi* 气) and then into spirit. Creating an immortal embryo within, they find mystical oneness with Dao and ascend spiritually into the heavens.

Complete Perfection lineages include not only those founded by the Seven Perfected but, after the school's ascent to central political status, also many other, traditional and local Daoist groups. Example are the Highest Clarity (Shangqing 上清) lineage centered on Maoshan 茅山 near Nanjing, the leading school of medieval Daoism, the Huashan 华山 line near Xi'an, and various groups of lay priests who have formal standing within the school without belonging to a monastery. They each have developed their own unique training regimens, including specific forms of taiji quan and forms of internal cultivation.

YouTube: "UNCC: Interview with Daoist Monks"

Read: Eskildsen, Stephen. 2004. *The Teachings and Practices of the Early Quanzhen Taoist Masters*. Albany: State University of New York Press.

Komjathy, Louis. 2013. *The Way of Complete Perfection: A Quanzhen Daoist Anthology*. Albany: State University of New York Press.

Wong, Eva. 1990. *Seven Taoist Masters*. Boston: Shambhala

Yao, Ted. 2000. "Quanzhen—Complete Perfection." In *Daoism Handbook*, edited by Livia Kohn, 567-93. Leiden: Brill.

7. Levels of Priesthood

To become a Daoist in China today, in continuation of Wang Kunyang's codification, the adept first finds a local master, often living in a small temple. After some basic training and with family approval, he or she is officially adopted into a lineage. This involves an initiation ceremony with the transmission of sacred texts—including the *Daode jing* 道德经 (Book of the Dao and Its Power) with its major commentaries—a vow to continue the tradition, the acceptance of ten basic precepts, and the bestowal of a religious name.

All schools and lineages follow this system, monastic practitioners typically joining a celibate institution, while lay priests continue to have families and work within their communities. Depending on the lineage chosen, each specializes in certain kinds of texts, rituals, and practices. Encouraged to look further afield, many decide to study with various teachers, and some become holders of multiple lineages.

Beyond this, monastic adepts can move to an advanced level, traditionally divided into two steps of 180 and 300 precepts respectively but today merged into one rank. Selected upon recommendation of their home temples and after passing an extensive central examination, they train at the Chinese Daoist Academy (Zhongguo daojiao xueyuan 中國道教學院). Sponsored and run by the Chinese Daoist Association, it was first established in 1990 at the White Cloud Temple in Beijing as a seminary for monks. A second center, also for males, was founded in 2010 on Mount Qingcheng 青城山 in Sichuan. Since 2005, nuns have been able to undergo advanced training at a facility located at the foot of Nanyue 南岳 (Hunan), the sacred mountain of the south near Changsha.

At either place, the course lasts two years, with classes of 50-100 students. The curriculum closely matches traditional Chinese education, being broadly oriented toward cultivating the whole person, not only conveying knowledge but also mental, spiritual, and physical discipline. Students are taught many subjects, including Chinese culture, foreign languages, and temple administration, as well as Daoist history, ritual, music, literature, thought, taiji quan, internal cultivation, and more.

While including practical, modern subjects like computer skills and business management, the training remains strongly focused on traditional values and methods. In this respect, it stands in stark contrast to the narrow focus of lay Chinese education, which is almost entirely modeled on Western systems and sees success only in achieving good test results. The strong emphasis on the official doctrine of the Party, however, which still teaches that religion is an opiate for the people and will eventually be overcome by the ultimate Communist society, creates a detachment in graduates toward their own tradition, often making them into apparatchiks rather than spiritual representatives.

After passing the relevant examinations, graduates undergo advanced ordination to receive further texts and extensive precepts, often a major central ceremony held at the White Cloud Temple. They then typically return to their home institutions and take on the responsibilities of managing them in a modern way. Some also remain in the capital and work for the Chinese Daoist Association or in government agencies. Usually aged between 21 and 35, the newly trained elite is set to become a vigorous force promoting the Party-approved development of Daoism in future decades.

YouTube: "Becoming a Taoist Monk with Monk Yunrou"

Read: Herrou, Adeline. 2013. *A World of Their Own: Monastics and Their Community in Contemporary China*. St. Petersburg, Fla: Three Pines Press.

Kohn, Livia. 2004. *Cosmos and Community: The Ethical Dimension of Daoism*. Cambridge, Mass.: Three Pines Press.

8. The Kundao Curriculum

Moving beyond conventional gender distinctions, Daoist monastics no longer think of themselves as men and women and instead call themselves "Heaven Dao" (*qiandao* 乾道) and "Earth Dao" (*kundao* 坤道), adopting terms from the *Yijing* 易经 (Book of Changes). In their community living, they make no difference among male and female ranks, status, activities, or clothing. Both pursue the same goals, undergo the same training and ordination, participate equally in community tasks, and attain the same ranks.

The women's academy thus offers the same comprehensive curriculum as that designed for monks. Their two years or four semesters of courses divide into three general categories: Basic Cultural Education (*wenhua ke* 文化课), Religious Studies (*zongjiao ke* 宗教课) and Daoist Practices (*daojiao xiuchi* 道教修持).

"Basic Cultural Education" comprises eight subjects: Chinese Language (4 semesters), Political Thought (4 semesters), Chinese History (4 semesters), Classical Architecture (4 semesters), English (3 semesters), Chinese Calligraphy (3 semesters), Computer Skills (2 semesters), and Basic Accounting (1 semester).

"Religious Studies" has fifteen subjects: History of Daoism (4 semesters), taiji quan (4 semesters), Classics (2 semesters), Daoist Rituals (2 semesters), Daoist Music (2 semesters), *Zhuangzi* (2 semesters), *Yijing* (2 semesters), *Heshang gong*'s *Commentary on the Daode jing* (1 semester), *Daode jing* (1 semester), Daoist Art (1 semester), Daoist Regulations (1 semester), Temple Management (1 semester), Daoist Ethics (1 semester), Daoist Cultivation (1 semester) and Daoist Immortals (1 semester).

"Daoist Practices" incorporates three aspects over two years: Cultivation of Character, Daoist Customs, and Morning and Evening Services. All these courses are required for every student, and all students follow the same schedule. There is only one elective: learning to play a musical instrument. Every student must play at least one instrument, but each student can choose which one to learn.

The twenty-five classes are taught by a wide range of faculty. Some are Daoist practitioners from other temples in various regions. Others are experts or scholars of specific fields and work at nearby universities. For example, Professor Lü Xichen, a scholar of Daoist cultivation at Central Chinese Normal University, has taught the course on Daoist Ethics several times at the Kundao Academy. Her lectures center on the Daoist value system and analyze its forms and changes through history. As she notes, the difference between the renunciants and her students in the city are two: Daoists tend to be much more conscientious and hard-working than college or even graduate students; however, their initial level of education is quite low.

In addition, Daoist students also practice calligraphy every day for the entire two years. At the end of program, they publish a hand copied version of the *Daode jing* in Chinese brush work, each student contributing at least one chapter. It is usually a fine and artistic production. Beyond that, each student has to write a substantial graduation thesis that examine various topics, from philosophy through literature and cultivation to modern social and business issues.

YouTube: "Daoist Nun Wushu Demo"

Read: Wang, Robin R. 2009. "To Become a Female Daoist Master: Kundao in Training." In *Internal Alchemy: Self, Society, and the Quest for Immortality*, edited by Livia Kohn and Robin R. Wang, 165-80. Magdalena, NM: Three Pines Press.

9. Personal Attraction

There were no advanced Daoist ordinations from the mid-1930s to the 1990s, a sixty-year hiatus. Especially after 1949, all religious activity was restricted, coming to a complete stop during the Cultural Revolution. Practitioners were forcefully returned to the laity, having to work in fields or factories, and many had to get married and raise families. Reemerging after 1978, Daoists have worked hard to regain their standing, recover their land, and rebuild their institutions.

Since then, the number of Daoists on all levels has increased dramatically, and today religious institutions attract more and more young people. During times of economic insecurity in the 1990s, many joined for the regular stipend plus room and board the temple offered, although they may also have felt a general attraction to Daoist teachings and had some contact with one or the other practitioner. Typically, they did not know a great deal about Daoism when they chose to enter the monastery and learned on the job.

In the 2000s and with increased economic prosperity, the motivations changed. While some still see the monastic life as a solution to various problems they face in lay society, young people now may join because they are tired of the hustle and bustle of lay society, the rushing after more and more money and material goods. They want to pursue meaning in their lives and find inner serenity and peace of mind, lead a life of solitude and quietness, with a sense of fulfillment in their souls and a reconnection to nature and a simpler and more elementary life.

China today faces a spiritual vacuum, since Communist doctrines no longer match rapid economic development, increased prosperity, modern living, and the widening gap in wealth and social standing. The pursuit of material wealth and the capitalist worship of money can only provide life satisfaction so far, and especially people who find themselves in prosperous circumstances begin to look further afield.

As a result, there is an increasing number of millennials who desire to get away from the fast pace of life in an increasingly urbanized and polluted environment. Growing up in a technological and modern society fed by largely Western perspectives, they find themselves adrift and without a deep cultural identity or system of faith. Often feeling hemmed in by the requirements and daily routines of city life, they become curious about the traditional values of Chinese culture and seek out its spiritual ideals and practices.

Leaving society behind, they may join a Daoist temple or escape into nature, following the models of ancient immortals and timeless hermits. Living in caves or straw huts in mountain wilderness far away from civilization, they engage in qigong, meditation, hiking, and local exploration, leading a relaxed and simple life that may lack many modern conveniences but is free from desires and close to nature, allowing them to reconnect with a deeper level of themselves—in many ways recovering the original Daoist impulse and continuing the hermit traditions of the millennia, albeit with cell phone coverage and postings on social media.

YouTube: "Summoning the Recluse"

Read: Porter, Bill. 1993. *The Road to Heaven: Encounters with Chinese Hermits*. San Francisco: Mercury House.

10. Tourism

Ordinary people, unlike dedicated Daoists or hermits, typically come into contact with the religion as tourists. The rise in economic prosperity and easing of travel restrictions, combined with vast improvements in infrastructure—highways, high-speed rail, and airports that make temples and mountains easily accessible—have led to a massive increase in both domestic and international tourism. Once sleepy villages and remote mountain temples—now accessible by rope ways and cable cars—have morphed into bustling centers, complete with high-rise hotels, restaurants, souvenir shops, and tour companies. People also have more free time at their disposal, and especially the two week-long holidays around Chinese New Year (in February) and Founding Day (October 1) see millions of people traveling to a vast variety of destinations.

Not only have the Chinese taken to traveling more, but there has also been a great rise in the numbers of overseas Chinese and international visitors. They often but not necessarily rely on organized tours, some coming specifically in search of Daoist spirituality. With this change, Daoist institutions have come to be supervised not only by the Bureau of Religious Affairs but also the Department of Tourism. Manned by foreign-oriented and modern-minded officials, the Department is interested mainly in revenue and the smooth entertainment of large crowds. It has little or no concern for religious activities or the creation of a spiritual atmosphere.

The effect of this multiple administration is twofold. On the one hand, the two agencies tend to squabble over money, and if one gets more from a temple activity than the other, they alert the police and accuse the monks of nefarious activities. On the other hand, they channel state and tourist funds toward restoration and expansion, so that many Daoist sanctuaries now have a revived and energized look, are open to the public, and offer a wide variety of Daoist resources, notably books, charms, herbs, teas, and martial training.

There is great regional variation in the degree of support and cooperation between these agencies and Daoist institutions. In some areas (Sichuan, Hubei), the local government makes Daoists very welcome and supports religious activities and festivals with enthusiasm. In others (Shaanxi, Shandong, Hunan), the politicians are wary of religious organizations and a restrictive mode prevails.

While temples used to be supported by donations from local communities, today the market economy and profit-driven tourism create various difficulties. Temples often have to compete with local travel bureaus, which turn mountains into so-called scenic areas. They then charge large entrance fees that are divided among the local government, the Daoist Association, and other official agents, leaving only a small portion for the Daoists and making worshipers less inclined to donate. In order to survive, Daoist temple leaders must learn the skills of contemporary management and apply them in a religious context.

While Daoists have always been good at adapting to changing times, today economic development is the primary force to determine its future direction. Temples have to maximize their resources and stimulate financial growth through multiple layers of business and commercial activities. For example, most temples today are also hotels that provide local cuisine and accommodations for tourists at reasonable prices. Many Daoists work in these businesses as cooks, waitresses, and entertainers. Popular fortune tellers charge fees to clients for discussion of their present and future, while priests perform rites geared to customers' unique needs.

The commercialization of temples inevitably brings about a more corporate-like structure of administration, replacing the traditional relationship of master and disciples. Temples are now often administered by a board of directors, leading to the formation of inner circles. While this brings about stability and continuity of leadership, it can also cause divisions and corruption, an overall lessening of the religious spirit underlying the Daoist commitment.

YouTube: "Are Chinese Tourists Actually THAT Bad?"

Read: Palmer, David A., and Elijah Siegler. 2017. *Dream Trippers: Global Daoism and the Predicament of Modern Spirituality*. Chicago: University of Chicago Press.

11. Sacred Mountains

Tourists tend to be particularly drawn to the major sacred mountains of China, representing the four cardinal directions and the center. Chinese cosmology postulates that the earth is flat and square, covered by the round, all-embracing canopy of the sky or heaven—giving it the overall shape of a turtle. Within this framework, the heavenly dome is held up by five major pillars: these are the five sacred mountains who, while consisting of multiple peaks, tend to rise rather steeply from the surrounding plains.

They all have leading mountain gods, closely embedded in the supernatural hierarchy under the rule of the Jade Emperor. Serving in various celestial departments, these deities outrank those of lesser peaks and social organizations such as cities, just as the Dragon King of the Eastern Sea, the chief officer in charge of water and rain making, is higher in status that his counterparts in rivers and lakes.

The five sacred mountains have long played an important role in imperial ritual. A most potent sign for an emperor having achieved cosmic harmony was his performance of the Feng and Shan sacrifices on Mount Tai, the sacred peak of the east. In Daoism, the five are further represented by cosmic talismans, the most potent among many divine charts and diagrams for various geographical locations. Just as maps were magical in the old days, bestowing control over the land to their owner, so the talismans of the five sacred mountains grant cosmic power over the country.

More specifically, Mount Tai 泰山 in the east (elev. 1545 m), near Confucius's birthplace in Qufu 曲阜 (Shandong), has traditionally been the realm of the dead, lorded over and judged by its deity, the Lord of Mount Tai (Taishan fujun 泰山府君). Numerous bamboo slips found in tombs from the Han dynasty onward contain petitions addressed to him as much as other Daoist gods, including lists of grave goods and presents to be given to the responsible otherworldly bureaucrats. His daughter, moreover, is the Goddess of the Morning Clouds (Bixia yuanjun 碧霞元君), a popular Daoist deity who brings children, prosperity, and good fortune.

Mount Song 嵩山 in the center (elev. 1440 m), located near Luoyang 洛阳 (Henan), honors a variety of Daoist saints and historical heroes, but is better known for being close to the center of Buddhist martial arts, the Shaolin Temple 少林寺. Here various academies train children and youngsters in all sorts of acrobatics and martial arts, enabling them to serve as artists, body guards, and even film stars.

Mount Hua 华山 in the west (elev. 2200 m), about 80 miles east of Xi'an 西安, with its highly dangerous five scraggly peaks—now accessible by cable car—is famous for being the home of the Hairy Lady (Maonü 毛女), a lady at the court of the First Emperor who fled into the mountains and became immortal, discovered several centuries later and duly killed by civilization. In addition, it housed the early Song master Chen Tuan 陈抟 (d. 989), famed physiognomist and imperial adviser, who developed ecstatic shamanic journeys called "sleep exercises."

Mount Heng 恒山 in the north (elev. 2017 m), near Datong 大同 (Shanxi), known for temples hanging improbably from steep cliffs, provided refuge to the Tang immortal Zhang Guolao 张果老, a member of the Eight Immortals who excelled in magic, herbalism, and martial arts and is best known for riding backwards on his donkey.

The other Mount Heng 衡山 in the south (elev. 1290 m), near Changsha 长沙 (Hunan), finally, is where the immortal lady Wei Huacun 魏华存 (251-334) lived in seclusion. A senior leader of the early Celestial Masters, she perfected personal cultivation and ascended to the heavens, from where she appeared to the medium Yang Xi in the 360s, providing key information on the newly discovered heaven of Highest Clarity and thus becoming a major revelatory deity of this school. Her independence and spiritual prowess has inspired numerous Daoist women, and the Kundao Academy is close to her sanctuary.

With high-speed train stations nearby and roadways as well as cable cars making even high peaks accessible, these five have become top religious tourist destinations. They all charge an entrance fee at their base, which go to the Department of Tourism, as well as money for specific temples and overnight stays that remain with the Daoists. Roadside shrines are shared by vendors, and scenic restaurants complete the scene.

YouTube: "Journey to Hua Shan"

"Mount Taishan"

Read: Hahn, Thomas H. 2000. "Daoist Sacred Sites." In *Daoism Handbook*, edited by Livia Kohn, 683-707. Leiden: Brill.

Robson, James 2009. *Power of Place: The Religious Landscape of the Southern Sacred Peak in Medieval China*. Cambridge, Mass: Harvard University Asia Center.

12. Daoist Sites

In addition to the five sacred peaks, tourists also flock to the numerous specifically Daoist mountains, found all over China. There monks and nuns are busily building or rebuilding temples, working hard to set up an increasingly tourist-friendly infrastructure.

The most prominent among these sites tend to be associated with the founding of major schools, commemorating the revelation of Daoist scriptures to leading masters. Among the earliest is the appearance of Lord Lao, the divinized Laozi, to Zhang Daoling 张道陵 in 142 CE, which led to the founding of the Celestial Masters (Tianshi 天师), still strong in Taiwan and southeast China. The event occurred in Sichuan in the southwest, and several mountains claim the honor, most importantly Qingcheng shan 青城山 and Heming shan 鹤鸣山.

Qingcheng shan is only a short high-speed train ride from Chengdu and receives the bulk of visitors. Besides the prominent Tianshi dong 天师洞 (Celestial Master's Cave), a large monastery a short walk up the hill, it has a flourishing hotel community at its base, sports a gigantic statue of Lord Lao on the central peak, offers accommodation and restaurants at the top, and is easily accessible by cable car. It is also the site of the second major Daoist Academy run by the Daoist Association.

Heming shan, in contrast, is more laid back, an active community of monks and nuns that receives few visitors, whose buildings were badly damaged in the 2008 earthquake. To encourage more tourists, the local authorities have created a new version of the site on a nearby hill, with big and modern but largely empty worship halls, a few talisman and souvenir stands, plus a prominent vegetarian Daoist restaurant nearby. This arrangement allows the religious practitioners to pursue their cultivation while tourists get to see a modern, sanitized version of the compound.

A second Daoist revelation took place in the 360s on Maoshan near Nanjing, when various immortals such as Wei Huacun connected to the medium Yang Xi, hired by the aristocratic Xu family to inquire about the fate of their ancestors. They described in detail the heaven of Highest Clarity and its illustrious denizens and also provided meditation and practice instructions that allowed dedicated practitioners to communicate with and eventually become one of them.

Maoshan was badly damaged during the Cultural Revolution and recovered slowly, its two sides following rather different economic models. Monks on the north side toward the district center of Jurong 句容 closely worked with the authorities and attracted large amounts in investment. They encouraged the creation of a natural park or "scenic area," erected a gigantic Lord Lao on the top, and sponsored various health enhancement ventures, overall vigorously commercializing the site.

The nuns on the south side, in contrast, focused more on religious and cultivation practices. Refusing to take entrance fees or accept state-sponsored funding, they instead attracted private donors and put Daoist culture on the map by training a music troupe that rose to great renown. Their halls are less ostentatious and more spiritually potent or "numinous" (*ling* 灵), they provide fewer tourist facilities, and generally attract a clientele that is more thoughtful and devout.

YouTube: "Mount Qingcheng and Dujiangyan"

Read: Johnson, Ian. 2012. "Two Sides of a Mountain: The Modern Transformation of Maoshan." *Journal of Daoist Studies* 5:89-116.

13. Laozi

Other major Daoist sites center on the alleged author of the *Daode jing*, the semi-legendary figure of Laozi 老子, later to be identified with Dao itself and divinized as Lord Lao, rising eventually to the status of leading deity and becoming a member of the Three Pure Ones.

Early sources describe him as having lived in the 6th century BCE, born as Li Er 李耳 or Li Dan 李旦 in Bozhou 亳州 in eastern Henan. Serving as an official scribe under the Zhou dynasty, he had both eminent knowledge of the rites and strong reclusive tendencies. Confucius heard of him and went to learn his teaching. Despite being rebuffed, he came away with a deep impression and great admiration. According the *Shiji* (Historical Records), he told his disciples,

> Birds, I know, can fly; fish, I know, can swim; animals, I know, can run. For the running one can make a net; for the swimming one can make a line; for the flying one can make an arrow. But when it comes to the dragon, I have no means of knowing how it rides the

> wind and the clouds and ascends into heaven. Today I have seen Laozi who really is like upon a dragon.

Later, so the story continues, when Laozi felt that the dynasty was declining, he left China for the western lands and was stopped by the border guard Yin Xi 尹喜, who had spotted the sage's unique energy from his lookout tower and asked him to transmit his ideas, then compiled them into the *Daode jing*. A medieval expansion of the story has Yin Xi beg the sage to take him along on his travels. However, Laozi denies the request and tells him to practice self-cultivation and chant the *Daode jing* 10,000 times over a three-year period, then meet up with him further west in Sichuan. He was to look for the sign of a black sheep (*qingyang* 青羊) for sale in the market of Chengdu, and follow its owner home, where Laozi would be staying.

According to the myth, all this came to pass, and the two sages set off toward the west, where they underwent a series of ordeals, reminiscent of the myth of the hero, and finally succeeded in "coverting the barbarians" (*huahu* 化胡), leading to the rise of an Indian version of the religion, identified as Buddhism.

Beyond these tales connected to the semi-historical Laozi, Daoist doctrine has him appear numerous times in the world, beginning with the very creation of the universe, where he emerged as the pure power of Dao. He guided the world through all the major stages of cultural development by appearing as sagely imperial adviser. In living history, moreover, he manifested in various miraculous appearances to emperors and leading Daoists, indicating his approval of certain reigns and policies. Beyond all this, Laozi is also credited with a variety of healing and meditation exercises as well as with the rescue and protection of people in need.

YouTube: "Eastern Philosophy:Laozi"

"Laozi chuguan"

Read: Kohn, Livia. 1998. *God of the Dao: Lord Lao in History and Myth*. University of Michigan, Center for Chinese Studies.

14. New Expansions

All the major sites connected to events in Laozi's life have long been honored with temples, statues, and inscriptions. Thus, his birthplace in Bozhou, now located in a town called Luyi 鹿邑 on the Anhui-Henan border, is the site of a major temple, the Taiqing gong 太清宫 (Great Clarity Palace), built around one of the oldest Daoist steles, the *Shengmu bei* 圣母碑 (Holy Mother Stele), erected in honor of Laozi's mother in 153 CE.

The place where Yin Xi spotted the sage and the *Daode jing* was transmitted is known as the Louguantai 楼观台 (Lookout Tower), an old monastic complex about 80 miles southwest of Xi'an. The area also housed the largest state-sponsored Daoist monastery of the Tang dynasty, the Zongsheng guan 宗圣观 (Temple of the Ancestral Sage).

The meeting place in the market of Chengdu, finally, grew into a major sanctuary, named Qingyang gong 青羊宫 (Black Sheep Palace) after the sign of the ram. In the Qing dynasty, the site was expanded to house the Erxian'an 二仙庵 (Two Immortals' Hermitage), dedicated to Lü Dongbin and Han Xiangzi 韩箱子 of the Eight Immortals. Traditionally a state-sponsored center for the printing and distribution of Daoist scriptures, it still houses the original woodblocks of the Ming-dynasty Daoist canon.

While all three were greatly reduced during the Cultural Revolution, they have seen an unprecedented revival, leading not only to the restoration of the original temples but also to the creation of extensive exhibition areas and archaeological parks. Historically accurate and built in cooperation with top scholars at leading universities, they include the life-sized model of a Warring States village, at Luyi, the compete reconstruction of the Tang complex next to Louguantai, and a major Culture Park in Chengdu.

While this development enhances Daoism and recovers history, it also has a shadow side, most obvious in other cultural construction that often puts life-sized replicas of world-famous monuments into Chinese cities or parks in a new form of architecture known as "duplitecture." For example, Hangzhou sports a White House, an Eiffel Tower, and a Venetian residential compound. while Suzhou has fifty-six replicas of famous bridges, including those at the Tower of London, Sydney harbor, and the Seine in Paris.

Typically, such projects require that villages or city quarters be razed and populations relocated, a feature possible only through the close cooperation and even collusion between Party executives, officials, and business men. This, then, is one area where big money meets official corruption, a manifestation of what is known as crony capitalism, the dominant form of doing business in China today.

Government officials, in close connection to Party secretaries, have unlimited control over real estate, state owned enterprises, and positions in the local administration, and essentially all of these are for sale at the right price and for people with the right connections. More specifically a local entrepreneur might bribe an influential politician or Party member by sending cash in red envelopes, commonly given at major festivals such as New Year's.

He or she would then be appointed to an office with impact in the area of his business, enabling him to steer regulations and state funds into a favorable direction, making a profit of several hundred percent. Another scheme is the forced repossession of land, which the state legally owns, by local officials for resale to developers, again at a huge profit. Ordinary people are quite helpless in this process and have to accept the—often pitiful—recompensation and/or relocation, lest they be forcefully removed or even killed by the local police under orders from the government.

Daoist redevelopment, while for the most part run by and for the Daoists themselves, has not been exempt from this ubiquitous pattern, and especially the large-scale construction of archaeological parks—with Disney-style rides and high entrance fees—do less for the religion than the business world.

YouTube: "LouGuang Tai"

Read: Pei, Minxin. 2016. *China's Crony Capitalism*. Cambridge, Mass: Harvard University Press.

Schmitz, Rob. 2016. *Street of Eternal Happiness: Big City Dreams along a Shanghai Road*. New York: Crown Publishers, chs. 2, 10.

15. Public Spectaculars

Another way in which scenic spots, and therefore also Daoist mountains, are increasing tourist revenue is by staging public spectaculars, what the Chinese call "large-scale musical dramas performed in real landscape settings" (*daxing shanshui shijing yinyue ju* 大型山水实景音乐剧).

Essentially organizers take a scenic spot, usually a flat area or body of water flanked by hillsides or mountains, and set up a stand of bleachers, mostly in the open, but some under a wooden or metal roof. They then stage elaborate performances, always at night time, with spectacular light and special effects, that involve various levels of music, singing, dance, and acrobatics—performers appearing at odd times in odd places, rising up from the ground or the water, swooping down from the mountain side, or popping up from behind boulders and temple buildings.

Themes involve local tales and represent the specific activities or traditions of the area, so that, for example, the performance on Mount Tianmen in Hunan tells the story of a divine fox lady who entices innocent young scholars with her wiles. Near the sacred mountain of the center, the spectacular involves large numbers of Shaolin monks who demonstrate both their devotional and martial activities to the accompaniment of Buddhist-inspired songs.

A performance I watched near Laojun shan 老君山, a mountain dedicated to Lord Lao south of Luoyang, showed various Daoist themes, including creation from chaos and the ascent of flying immortals.

Public spectaculars in many ways are the pinnacle of the "Disneyfication" of traditional Chinese culture and religion, coming right after the use of Daoism to construct characters and plots in Hong Kong horror and martial arts movies like "Crouching Dragon Hidden Tiger" and "A Chinese Ghost Story." Here heroes somersault at will and fly through the air, activate potent talismans and chant lines from the *Daode jing* to make themselves invulnerable in battle. They vanquish supernatural man-eating wolves in the forest, overcome the powers of tree monsters, exorcise ghosts from deserted temples, and even descend into the depths of hell, confronting powerful dark forces rescuing and their hapless victims. Mediating between humans and spirits, between the living and the dead, Daoist-inspired heroes, using ritual and other means, help innocents to recover their lives and honor their ancestors.

In addition, there are comparatively tame historical dramas that retell major Daoist myths and legends, such as stories of the Eight Immortals and the movie rendition of Laozi's life, *Laozi chu Hangu guan* 老子出函谷关 (Laozi Emigrated through the Hangu Pass), both with English subtitles. Altogether, these various venues ensure the continued vibrant presence of Daoism in popular culture, making optimal use of the entertainment value especially of its more supernatural and magical aspects.

YouTube: "Shaolin yinyue"

Read: Cahill, Suzanne. 2011. "What to Fear and How to Protect Yourself: Daoism and Hong Kong Horror Movies." *Journal of Daoist Studies* 4:202-18.

16. Martial Arts

The Hong Kong film industry is also responsible for the massive rise in martial arts at religious institutions on the mainland, starting in the late 1980s, when movie makers began to hire talent, especially from the academies at the Shaolin Temple. This precipitated the reconstruction of the monastery, which had been completely razed by local warlords in the 1920s, and the establishment of more martial arts schools. Daoists, too, were inspired to recover and expand their own version of martial training, documented since the middle ages. Soon each mountain lineage began to promote its particular style and brand.

Martial arts in general are a form of physical practice geared toward fitness and self-defense in combination with ethical principles. They inherit two traditional value systems: ancient Confucian chivalry, which encouraged the practice of archery and charioteering as tools for aristocratic self-cultivation and emphasized honor, respect, good manners, precise timing, balance, and composure in all actions; plus traditional Daoist concepts of bending and softness, which stressed flexibility, yielding, humility, nonviolence, inner focus, and wisdom.

Martial practice divides into hard and soft or outer and inner, forms. That is, the hard forms focus on muscle and strength building, teach fighting techniques, and work toward defeating the opponent. Soft forms, in contrast, encourage internal awareness and have healing and even spiritual benefits.

The dominant Daoist form is taiji quan 太极拳 (Great Ultimate Boxing), which allegedly began in the Ming dynasty when the Daoist immortal Zhang

Sanfeng 张三丰 looked out the window of his hermitage on Mount Wudang 武当山 and saw a crane fighting with a snake. The two animals turned and twisted in a complex pattern, neither gaining advantage yet matching the cosmic interaction of yin and yang. Imitating their movements, he created the first sequence of the practice, which he later—together with other movement patterns, a collection of poetry, and his complete autobiography—channeled to the Sichuan Daoist Li Xiyue 李西月 (1806-1856). Zhang in due course became the patron saint of the practice; he is also the main link to Daoism which—however much it may have favored martial practices—originally had no part in its development.

Historically taiji quan began with the military general Chen Wangting 陈王廷 (1580-1660) who, after fighting the Manchu conquest in the 1630s, retired to his hometown and began to teach martial exercises consisting of five routines and a sequence of 108 moves. Transmitted through the family, his methods were organized into a slightly less martial system by his descendant Chen Zhangxing 陈长兴 (1771-1853), leading to what is today known as the Chen-style, a series of moves in the four directions.

Yang-style, on the other hand, goes back to Yang Luchan 杨露禅 (1799-1872), who originally studied Shaolin boxing, then became a student of Chen Zhangxing. His practice is softer and rounder, with wide arm movements, circular patterns, and intricate flexing in the wrists and arms. Spread by his sons and developed further into various sub-lineages, it is the most popular form of taiji quan today. The name, moreover, goes back to Neo-Confucian and *Yijing* cosmology and their emphasis on the notion of the Great Ultimate, symbolized in moving clouds and eventually in the well-known diagram, which appeared first in 1613.

Taiji quan is executed from a standing position and involves continuous movements that are choreographed into lengthy and complex sequences. In both its basic, unarmed and variant forms (with sword, fan, stick, or pole), it eschews the development of large muscles and powerful strength in favor of internal suppleness (*jin* 筋), a springiness in tendons, sinews, and ligaments.

Rather than using the mind to systematically guide *qi* (as in qigong, used mainly for healing), practitioners keep it open and relaxed, allowing the *qi* to flow smoothly in all directions and the spirit to be receptive to all stimuli. The practice combines an open and relaxed meditative awareness with soft, slow, and focused body movements; its overall goal is to flow along with the Dao at creation in a smooth, supple, and relaxed way. Taiji quan is thus both a spiritual and martial practice and today forms the foundation of Daoist training all over China.

YouTube: "Wudang Taoist Kung Fu Academy Performance"

"Chinese Wudang Kung Fu"

Read: Bidlack, Bede. 2006. "Taiji Quan: Forms, Visions, and Effects." In *Daoist Body Cultivation*, edited by Livia Kohn, 179-202. Magdalena, NM: Three Pines Press.

17. Mount Wudang

The leading location of Daoist martial arts is Mount Wudang, where Zhang Sanfeng allegedly observed the fighting animals. Already a religious center in the Tang, it became a major Daoist sanctuary in the early Ming dynasty, when it was associated with protecting the imperial house and served as the main worship place of the Perfect Warrior (Zhenwu 真武).

Originally called Dark Warrior (Xuanwu 玄武), indicating a constellation in the northern sky, and depicted as an intertwined turtle and snake, this figure soon appeared as a mighty warrior. His rise to imperial protector began in the Song, when he was seen as the latent force behind the universe and was associated with potent protector deities of tantric background. A national cult developed, he appeared in various manifestations at court, was honored in inscriptions and records, and his hagiography grew to ever longer accounts of miraculous lives and military exploits.

The Ming rulers set up regular sacrifices for him and between 1405 and 1418 greatly expanded his center on Mount Wudang. Bolstered by imperial patronage, the god was adopted by both leading Daoist schools, Complete Perfection and Celestial Masters, and he grew into an increasingly popular figure. He also became the protector of Daoist martial arts, described vividly in the late-Ming novel *Fengshen yanyi* 封神演义 (Creation of the Gods), where Lord Lao appears variously to fight for the righteous, give advice, provide weapons, and mastermind battle plans.

Located northwest of Wuhan, the capital of Hubei, Mount Wudang consists of multiple peaks, each covered by Daoist temples, today encompassing fifty-three ancient buildings and nine architectural sites. The highest and most important is Jinding 金顶 (Golden Peak), accessible by cable car, with its elaborate temple complex and crowning statue of the Perfect Warrior, made from bronze and weighing about two tons.

The other major temple is the Zixiao gong 紫霄宫 (Palace of the Purple Clouds), which covers an area of two acres and includes numerous halls and shrines. Nearby, moreover, is the Nanyan gong 南岩宫 (Palace of the Southern Cliff), a set of buildings carved right into the steep cliff side. The entire range is a protected natural park under the auspices of the Department of Tourism and has been declared a UNESCO World Heritage Site in 1994.

A popular retreat for Westerners on Mount Wudang is the Wuxian guan 五仙观 (Monastery of the Five Immortals) on Baima shan 白马山 (White Horse Mountain). Run by Master Li 李 (b. 1964), an accomplished and widely trained Daoist master, it houses as many as thirty students who engage in various practices. They range from martial arts through scripture studies to various forms of internal cultivation, including internal alchemy (see http://fiveimmortals.com). As David Hessler, who took a two-week course there in 2017, notes in a personal email,

> Master Li was a good teacher. He did a nice job or explaining some complex ideas to Westerners. The students who had taken several classes from him loved him, including two long-term disciples. I learned a lot about the rituals to follow at a Daoist temple and found Master Li to be of good humor and exceptional understanding of Dao, as well as an inspiring practitioner of water and fire taiji quan and gongfu. I found immersing myself in a temple environment very beneficial.

YouTube: "3 Days in the Sacred Wudang Taoist Mountain"

Read: Chao, Shin-yi. 2011. *Daoist Rituals, State Religion, and Popular Practices: Zhenwu Worship from Song to Ming (960-1644)*. London: Routledge.

DeBernardi, Jean. 2010. "Wudang Mountain and the Modernization of Daoism." *Journal of Daoist Studies* 3:202-10.

Meulenbeld, Mark. 2015. *Demonic Warfare: Daoism Territorial Networks and the History of the Ming Novel*. Honolulu: University of Hawaii Press

18. Reaching Abroad

With increased economic prosperity and the drive toward world power, China has been expanding its influence abroad, focusing particularly but not exclusively on developing countries with great metal or mineral resources. Efforts are threefold: state-owned enterprises that strike deals with governments and provide aid, private conglomerates that set up cooperative ventures, and individual businessmen who establish their brands in various locations.

Used to their home-style brand of crony capitalism, Chinese entrepreneurs on all levels tend to be overbearing and arrogant, with little or no regard for local culture and customs. They impress leading magnates with grand projects and rich gifts, and expect exclusive contracts largely in their favor, typically hoping to build massive infrastructure projects (roads, railways, bridges, power plants) in exchange for the rights to mine metals or minerals the growing Chinese economy so urgently needs.

Geographically their prime focus has been Africa, where governments in numerous small states have struck big deals and where China is by far the largest foreign investor. This is followed closely by Central Asian countries in China's backyard, where the One Belt One Road initiative not only seeks to create easy lines of communication and transport but also to establish a solid Chinese presence. Beyond that, China has been very active cooperating with Australian mining operations and ruling elites in Polynesian islands as well as in Papua New Guinea and, to a lesser but not unimportant degree, in South America.

The Chinese government has also begun to establish port facilities that house military vessels officially serving as escorts through pirate-infested waters along the southern sea route toward the Middle East, its main supply line for oil. Notably the Strait of Malacca between Indonesia and Singapore forms a bottle neck that could be easily blocked by a hostile navy, bringing China's economy to a grinding halt within days.

The success rate of this expansion policy has been a great deal less than claimed in alarmist Western publications. Very little land in Africa is owned by Chinese, and agriculture plays a minimal role. Crony capitalism, too, only goes so far. Often the Chinese strike deals with authoritarian tyrants, only to find them toppled in an overthrow or ousted in an election, rendering their efforts null and void. The prime example here is Myanmar, where they were hand-in-glove with the ruling junta but have lost their influence since democratization.

Also, once actually in business, the Chinese tend to bring in their own workers and engineers as well as supply personnel. Treating locals as inferiors and refusing to train them, they never really benefit the local economy. This leads to high levels of resentment and may result in protests, in some cases causing projects to fold. Add to this the overall shoddy quality of their work—one road in Africa began to crumble at one end before it was completed at the other—and it becomes understandable that their overall success rate is maybe around 30 percent, for the most part being a massive waste of money.

Another major expense, meant to result in cultural rather than economic expansion, is the worldwide initiative of establishing so-called Confucius Institutes in cooperation with academic institutions. Not unlike the British Council or the Japan Foundation, these Institutes propose to increase access to Chinese learning, both of language and culture (http://english.hanban.org).

Typically, a full professor at the host institution serves as director, joined by a Chinese language instructor sent from headquarters in Beijing and helped by several local assistants. Each Institute operates independently, without thematic or ideological restrictions. They each receive an annual budget to cover salaries—especially for language teachers who work at the host institution and other venues, especially high schools—as well as for library acquisitions, workshop expenses, honoraria for guest speakers, and more. Often placed at less prominent universities and in more remote locations, the Institutes—so far around 500 worldwide—make an important contribution to the understanding of China worldwide while also aiding the government's expansive ambitions.

YouTube: "China's Global Domination Plan—One Belt, One Road"

Read: Brautigam, Deborah. 2015. *Will Africa Feed China?* New York: Oxford UP.

Economy, Elizabeth, and Michael Levi. 2014. *By All Means Necessary: How China's Resource Quest Is Changing the World.* New York: Oxford University Press.

French, Howard W. 2014. *China's Second Continent: How a Million Migrants are Building a New Empire in Africa.* New York: Vintage Books.

Miller, Tom. 2017. *China's Asian Dream.* London: ZED Books.

19. International Masters

As part of the overall Chinese reach abroad, Daoist organizations, too, are making more efforts to create positive relationships overseas and establish Daoist masters and centers abroad. Thus, for example, the Chinese Daoist Association every so often sends official delegations on tours to U. S. and Europe, hoping to connect to universities, overseas Chinese, and local practitioners.

Its vice chairman, the accomplished master and long-time hermit Meng Zhiling 孟至岭, moreover, runs regular workshops in the West. Addressing groups of about forty practitioners, he teaches different aspects of Daoist cultivation, including philosophy and ethics as well as taiji quan and quiet sitting meditation. In the U. S., he lectures near New York City, sponsored by the US Taoist Association (http:// ustaoistassoc.com/1.html), an unofficial arm of its Chinese counterpart run by David Hessler, who also leads the Society of Daofa ziran (http://societyofdaofaziran.com).

In addition, Master Meng is also active in the International Daoist Forum. Held in China every two-to-three years, it brings together practitioners and scholars from China and the West to engage in Daoist practice and discuss issues of Daoist teachings, such as the adaptation of key notions to the modern world.

Another, slightly less official, representative of Chinese Daoism is Master Chen (Zeng Yongxiang 曾永祥; www.wudangchen.com), a 25th generation Dragon Gate and 14th generation Zhang Sanfeng lineage holder, sent to the U. S. in 1990 to spread Daoism. Trained on Mount Wudang and teaching a mix of martial arts and internal alchemy, he built communities in various cities, notably New York, Atlanta, and St. Louis before settling in Colorado, where he now runs Dao House near Estes Park, a retreat center and starting point for a future Daoist temple.

President and founder of the Daoist Association USA (https://daousa.org) and the North American Wudang Daoist Association, he offers priestly training, spiritual counseling, various ceremonies to celebrate life events as well as protective devices, such as talismans. Every year, moreover, he sponsors the Universal Consciousness Festival, a Daoist gathering that provides workshops on Daoist living (https://www.universalconsciousnessfestival.org).

A yet different Daoist organization with an increasing foothold in the West is the Taoist Tai Chi Society (http://www.taoist.org/usa), the international arm of a major Hong Kong temple, known as Fung Loy Kok. It began when Master Moy Lin Shin emigrated for Canada in 1970 and from there spread throughout North America. With a dominant focus on the practice of its own unique brand of taiji quan, the Society emphasizes health benefits and moral values, allowing members to rise to higher levels but not initiating anyone into the Daoist priesthood. It has by far the most Western followers.

While there is a certain proselytizing fervor among all these masters, they tend to be sincere and honest and strive to present the tradition in an authentic way, emphasizing good ethics and purity of living besides health benefits and spiritual attainments.

YouTube: "Master Chen"

Read: Moretz, Harrison. 2009. "The Dao is Not for Sale." *Journal of Daoist Studies* 2:167-76.

Siegler, Elijah. 2007. *New Religious Movements.* Upper Saddle River, NJ: Prentice Hall.

20. Western Daoists

A yet different form of Daoist international expansion is the practice and teaching by Westerners initiated into the religion by Chinese masters in China, then building communities in their homeland. There are numerous such Western masters, prominent all over Europe and the U. S. I introduce a few representatives.

A major force in the initiation of western Daoists since the mid-1990s has been Feng Xingzhao, the abbot of a small, isolated temple called Leigutai 擂鼓台 (Terrace of Rolling Thunder) in the high mountains of southern Shaanxi near Ankang. He initiated many of the leading Daoists of Europe, including Shi Jing and his fellows of the British Taoist Association (http://www.taoists.co.uk); Karine Martin and other of the Association Française Daoiste whose center near Montluçon opened in 2017 (http://france-dao.blogspot.com); and Hervé Louchouarn, the leader of a Chinese medicine clinic and Daoist community in Guernavaca, Mexico (https://tusaludcuernavaca.wordpress.com/tag/prof-herve-louchouarn-t).

All these groups provide lessons in taijiquan and qigong, teach Daoist philosophy and ethics, offer healing and counseling, and operate Daoist temples and priestly education. They also commonly publish newsletters and sponsor workshops with leading Daoists, scholars, and taiji masters.

In the U. S., practicing Daoists tend to be initiated by various masters. For example, Michael Rinaldini, founder of the American Dragon Gate Lineage (http://qigongdragon.com) with a center in Santa Rosa, California, trained with Master Wan Sujian (b. 1953). A former military physician, he runs a medical qigong clinic on the outskirts of Beijing, which he expanded to also house a Daoist temple in 2002. Training in bagua and other forms of taijiquan as well as in medical qigong and Daoist scripture studies, Rinaldini practiced at home and visited Wan over several years. In 2003, he received formal initiation as a Daoist priest by Wan's resident Daoist. He now has an active training center and himself initiates the next generation

Louis Komjathy, the founder of the Daoist Foundation (http:// daoistfoundation.org), trained with Chen Yuming, a vice abbot on Huashan and lived both there and on Laoshan as a Daoist monk. He also holds a Ph. D. and serves as an academic professor of Daoist studies at the University of San Diego. At his center, he teaches various workshops and proposed an integrated program that encompasses a Daoist lifestyle (breathing, exercises, cooking, fengshui) in combination with internal cultivation and alchemical transformation.

Jerry Alan Johnson, the founder of the International College of Medical Qigong (http://www.medicalqigong.org), as well as his successor and the current director Bernard Shannon, in addition to training in traditional Chinese medicine and *qi*-healing, hold multiple Daoist lineages: Dragon Gate from Qingcheng shan in Sichuan, Highest Clarity from Maoshan near Nanjing, and Celestial Masters from Longhu shan in Jiangxi. The College is located in Palm Desert, California, complete with Chinese gardens and a Daoist sanctuary, the Temple of Peace and Virtue. In addition to training medical qigong healers, they also run a publishing house specializing in *qi*-healing, offer a program leading to initiation as a Daoist priest, and maintain continued close contact with Chinese masters.

YouTube: "Taoist Dragongate Discipleship"

"Daoist Bowing"

Read: http://www.taoists.co.uk/Files/FengXingzhao-interview.pdf

Komjathy, Louis. 2004. "Tracing the Contours of Daoism in North America." *Nova Religio* 8.2:5-27.

Palmer, David A., and Elijah Siegler. 2017. *Dream Trippers: Global Daoism and the Predicament of Modern Spirituality.* Chicago: University of Chicago Press.

Rinaldini, Michael. 2008. "How I Became a Daoist Priest." *Journal of Daoist Studies* 1:181-87.

Part 2

Economics

21. Economic Development

China is today the world's largest economy. This is the result of a massive expansion that increased it more than thirty-fold from $202 billion in 1980 to close to $7,000 billion in 2011. Growth rates—fueled by government credit, a controlled currency exchange rate, low-cost manufacturing, and global exports—stayed in the double digits for several decades and still hover around 7 percent. However, they are falling and expected to drop to 3-4 percent over the next few years. In addition, while the country's overall GDP is $11 trillion, its debt has risen to 260 percent of GDP, compared to 104 percent in the U.S.

China is far from a developed country. Per person GDP is $8,000, just above Peru. The income gap within the country is widening, as is the social divide, especially also under the impact of the Social Credit System. These days, China has the most billionaires after the U. S.: 1 percent of the population hold 30 percent of the country's wealth. About one third, 350 million, have reached the middle class, with annual incomes between $8,000 and $25,000. The remainder, 875 million, are still below, but set to move into cities and rise to the middle class in the near future, their incomes expected to rise by 15 to 20 percent.

These people make up the backbone of the Chinese economy. They are vibrantly entrepreneurial and aggressively upward moving. Many run sole proprietorships, and there are 40.6 million small businesses. When the government eased the requirement for cash reserves and simplified administrative procedures in 2015, new registrations rose dramatically. While moving the economy forward, the rising middle class will also require (and demand) expanding infrastructure and improved social services. This puts an additional burden on provincial and municipal governments, who are already facing heavy debt.

In addition, the economy is hampered by large-scale government interference, notably the state-owned enterprises that still control 40 percent of the economy and are known for being cumbersome, bureaucratic, and corrupt. In fact, they are a prime example of what economists Daron Acemoglu and James Robinson, in their ground-breaking study *Why Nations Fail*, call "extractive" as opposed to "inclusive" institutions.

> Extractive political institutions concentrate power in the hands of a narrow elite and place few constraints on the exercise of this power. Economic institutions are then often structured by this elite to extract resources from the rest of the society. The two are mutually interdependent: extractive economic institutions must inherently depend on extractive political institutions.
>
> Inclusive political institutions, on the other hand, vest power broadly, and tend to uproot economic institutions that appropriate the resources of many. . . They make it harder for others to usurp power and undermine the foundations, creating a more equitable distribution of resources and facilitating the persistence of inclusive political institutions. (2012, 81-82)

Extractive institutions prevent what economist Joseph Schumpeter has called "creative destruction," the way in which economic growth and technological change replace the old with the new. New firms take over, new technologies make existing skills and machines obsolete. The process creates losers as well as winners, endangers old privilege and power structures, potentially toppling governments and upending social patterns—in other words, it presents a major threat to Party rule.

This rule is still strong. Without an independent judiciary and unhindered by private competition, state-owned enterprises control entire industries, most importantly banking, transportation, telecommunications, the media, and real estate. The latter is a prime example on how local governments manipulate the economy, alternatively creating bubbles or slowing the market.

That is, they influence demand by willfully installing or removing home purchasing restrictions: preference to local versus out-of-town buyers, limits of the number of properties one can own, requirements on the amount of down payments, plus a wide variety of taxes due at purchase (in lieu of an annual property tax): value-added tax, land-value tax, real estate transaction tax, capital gains tax, property tax, education tax, to name but a few.

A rigged economy, combined with a lack of clear property laws and freedom of expression, does not bode well for China as it finds itself now in what economists call the middle-income trap. This is reached when a country has lost its competitive export edge due to rising wages and increased cost of living, yet is unable to evolve toward higher levels, mainly due to lack of creative destruction but also because of it fails to educate the people appropriately and does not create new opportunities for lower earners. In the 1960s, 106 countries entered the middle-income trap, and to date only thirteen have made it out—most notably Japan, South Korea, Singapore, and Taiwan, who all seriously democratized in the process and created excellent educational systems with justly enforced laws and free independent media.

YouTube: "The Middle Income Trap"

"Why Is the Chinese Economy Addicted to Debt?"

Read: Acemoglu, Daron, and James A. Robinson. 2012. *Why Nations Fail: The Origins of Power, Prosperity, and Poverty*. New York: Crown Publishers.

Rein, Shaun. 2014. *The End of Copycat China: The Rise of Creativity, Innovation, and Individualism in Asia*. New York: Wiley.

Shambaugh, David. 2016. *China's Future*. Cambridge: Polity Press.

22. City Temples

Daoist and other popular temples are part of the positive dynamic of the Chinese economy. Situated centrally in major cities, they are often the focus of commerce and the site of fairs and markets, plus they offer an opportunity to pray for protection and prosperity.

A prime example is the Chenghuang miao 城隍庙 (City God Temple) of Shanghai, smack in the middle of a vibrant tourism and shopping district called Yuyuan 豫园 (Pleasure Garden) after a beautiful Qing-dynasty garden, complete with ponds, bridges, pavilions, and rock formations. Pedestrian walkways meander among reconstructed traditional-style buildings housing all sorts of shops, from Starbucks through fashion accessories to souvenirs. Numerous stalls and vendors provide a mouth-watering selection of Shanghai street food, including cookies, buns, dumplings, and more.

The temple itself centers on a large open courtyard, where an incense burner smolders with numerous incense sticks. Various side halls, equipped with benches for kneeling and boxes for money offerings, worship a slew of Daoist and popular deities. The main hall is dedicated to Qin Yubo 秦羽博 (1295–1373), a local official under the Yuan dynasty and a distant relative of the late China scholar Julia Ching.

Having done much to ease the plight of citizens during his lifetime, after his death his spiritual energy was considered too potent to be limited to just his own family as an ordinary ancestor. Accommodating petitions by the local elite, the first emperor of the Ming Dynasty appointed him as city god. Believed to have greatly aided the city during times of crisis, notably in the 19th and 20th centuries under colonial rule and foreign occupation, by appearing to leading citizens in dreams and dispensing advice, he remained popular even after the founding of the People's Republic.

As China's economy expanded in the 19th century, the temple grew increasingly popular, offering an opportunity to express thanks and pray for good fortune. Expanding to include various side halls and niches of worship to other deities, it also housed regular fairs and became the center of a popular market with numerous local businesses setting up shop. In 1951, it was subsumed under the Shanghai Daoist Association and made into a Daoist center. As a result, statues representing folk deities and Buddhist figures were removed and more Daoist gods installed. Closed during the Cultural Revolution used for other purposes, it reopened in 1994 and was massively renovated in 2005-06.

Today, as much as many other city temples, the Shanghai temple is a popular destination for locals and tourists alike. It also contains a significant shrine to the God of Wealth, Guan Yu 关羽, originally a general from the Three Kingdoms period (221-265). In addition, it provides the opportunity to pray for positive interference by the divine functionary of one's year of birth. There are twelve such supernatural administrators, matching the animals of the Chinese zodiac and serving in of the Department of Destiny under the directorship of the Ruler of Fates (Siming 司命). In times of growing economic dynamic as well as insecurity, the City God Temple thus provides succor and spiritual support as well as the opportunity to pray for wealth, success, and personal good fortune.

YouTube: "City God Temple in Shanghai"

Read: Kohn, Livia. 1997. "The Taoist Adoption of the City God." *Ming Qing Yanjiu* 5:68-106.

23. Population Dynamics

With a population of 1.3 billion, China is the world's most populous country. Although today the median age is 37 years, the population is rapidly aging, so that citizens over 65, who numbered 100 million in 2005, will reach 330 million by 2050. Combined with a continuing low birth rate, this means that by then 44 percent of the population will not be of prime working age, placing a great burden of financial and social support on full-time workers and the state.

China was well on the way to lower birth rates and the two-child family in the 1950s, when Mao Zedong decreed that the country's true wealth lay in its people and ordered everyone to multiply as much as possible. This trend contributed to the overarching poverty encompassing the country and would have slowed quite naturally, once the edict was rescinded and economic progress commenced.

However, the Party, never content to leave well enough alone and in blatant opposition to the good old Daoist wisdom of nonaction, in 1980 instituted the one-child policy, imposing heavy fines on anyone daring to have a second or even third child. Local governments having to fulfill limiting quotas of childbirth took to harassing anyone resisting, from trashing their homes through taking their valuables to forcing women into (even late-term) abortions and involuntary sterilization.

Although rescinded now in favor a two-child model, the price has been high, especially since most of the population, still living in the countryside and following traditional forms of ancestor worship—however outlawed—saw a male heir as absolutely essential and either killed or abandoned females. Many Western families came to adopt a Chinese baby girl, often from legitimate orphanages but on occasion also as the result of human trafficking. Selling a girl abroad, after all, made it possible to pay the fine for the next try for a boy.

Population-wise, the policy has left China with a screwed gender ratio: while the normal rate is 103-108 males per every 100 females, in China it is as high as 118-120 in the countryside and about 110-112 in the cities. Not only creating a potential political powder keg, this has also made it difficult for men to find marriage partners, who often require not only a steady job but also home ownership and other assets before consenting to go on a date.

These are increasingly hard to come by as the Chinese education system is failing: unending memorization no longer cuts it in the rapidly shifting economy. Even college graduates, of whom there are more than ever before, often cannot find jobs. Having grown up in times of rising prosperity, they tend to have a sense of entitlement, wanting a cushy position with little effort and lots of money. Employers, on the other hand, are looking for people with real skills and creative thinking.

Another major factor in the population dynamics is the household registration (*hukou*) system, which firmly places each family in one particular location. While it is possible to travel to or even live in other places, anything requiring official involvement has to be done in one's hometown: health care, housing permit, driver's license, children's education, and more. As a result, huge numbers of people have become migrant workers (*liumin* 流民), living unregistered and without benefits in slums on the fringes of the big cities, making minimal wage and only seeing their families once or twice a year.

Some are well-educated but, as Liao Yiwu shows in the case of the village teacher Huang Zhiyuan, cannot make ends meet in their home town and move into the city. Unable to find legal employment, Huang worked in construction, and eventually ended up driving a flatbed tricycle. Even then, he was constantly on the run from police and on occasion faced imprisonment and had his vehicle impounded. Children suffer the most. If they stay at home, they have access to schooling and health care but grow up with grandparents or relatives. If they join their migrant parents, they have no schools to attend and grow up illiterate and unskilled, becoming part of a potentially explosive underclass that digs China deeper into the middle-income trap.

The government is set to alleviate this situation and has indicated easements in the registration system. It is also intent on urbanizing 300 million more people, moving them into newly build high-rises on the outskirts of smaller cities. These are typically created by developers, working hand-in-glove with local officials and concerned more with making money and showing commercial progress than with the needs of real people.

Not surprisingly, real people tend not to be too keen on these artificial monstrosities, especially when there are no jobs or facilities, leaving projects to turn into ghost cities—another huge expenditure with no return grown by crony capitalism.

A prime example of a ghost city in China is Chenggong, a satellite community about 20 minutes outside of Kunming, the capital of the southwestern province of Yunnan. Much of its newly constructed housing remains unoccupied, making it one of the largest ghost towns in Asia. Another is Dantu in Jiangsu, built in the early 2000s and only gradually attracting inhabitants now. Several cities, moreover, including Guangzhou and Shanghai, have built gigantic malls that remain unused or significantly underused. As larger segments of the population move into the middle class, it is hoped, these new ventures will attract businesses and become viable communities.

YouTube: "Why China's One-Child Policy Failed"

"The Chinese Hukou System"

"China Has a Crazy Number of Ghost Cities"

Read: Fong, Mei. 2016. *One Child: The Story of China's Most Radical Experiment*. Boston: Houghton Mifflin.

Liao, Yiwu. 2009. *The Corpse Walker: Real-Life Stories, China from the Bottom Up*. New York: Anchor, 160-72.

Schmitz, Rob. 2016. *Street of Eternal Happiness: Big City Dreams along a Shanghai Road*. New York: Crown Publishers, 134-40.

Shepard, Wade. 2015. *Ghost Cities of China*. London: Zed Books.

24. Temple Growth

The shift in population dynamics has made communities more vulnerable, loosening or dissolving traditional ties and shifting focus away from the extended family. As a result, many Chinese actively seek new forms of community, often turning to sports groups or clubs, but increasingly also discovering or recovering religious organizations to create social stability and support.

In this context, Daoist temples are becoming active community builders. Numerous in the old days, dotted across villages, towns, and mountains, with colorful frescoes, imposing statues, ornate furnishings, and gorgeous gardens, they were massively decimated after 1949 and completely eviscerated during the Cultural Revolution. Torturing leading monks as "rich land owners," as Liao Yiwu describes in his interview with the 103-year-old Buddhist abbot Deng Kuan, Red Guards would destroy paraphernalia and smash up statues, whitewash walls and spray-paint slogans, then turn the place over to the locals.

Many temples were completely razed, their building materials used by the peasants. The majority were reassigned, becoming military depots, kindergartens, or housing projects, their lands taken over by towns and local people, while monastics joined the laity or practiced in secrecy. Leaving the area or dying, few survivors remained, and some places have lost all memory of a temple's presence.

Thus, for example, the Daoist sanctuary to the Goddess of the Morning Clouds in Caishan 蔡山 near Xuzhou (Jiangsu) was discovered only after heavy rains in 2012 caused the roof to cave and plaster mud to wash away, uncovering murals concealed for decades.

Most temples' locations are known and, beginning in the mid-1980s, many have been rebuilt—leading to a three-fold increase in numbers over the last two decades. The process took many years of patient plodding, always respecting the population, honoring lay donors, cooperating with the authorities, and working very, very hard.

For example, when the first three monks returned to the Wengongci in Hanzhong, "the compound looked less like a temple than like an accumulation of houses without proper wall or context, singularly lacking in splendor" and partially occupied by lay families. However, the monks made it into a holy place through their vision: "They accurately described what had been there in the past and fervently outlined what they had planned for the future" (Herrou 2013, 2). This future, moreover, is not a mere replica of the past. Daoists rebuild differently, not only because the earlier forms are irretrievably lost, but also because they wish to transform and adapt the religion to the new century.

In this process, Daoist temples often become a pivot in community building. As Adeline Herrou shows in her amazing video, "Master Feng: A Daoist in China Today" (Paris: CNRS, 2017), Master Feng first returned to and restored his home temple, then assisted in the relocation and revitalization of a nearby city temple, and afterwards turned his attention on a largely ruined sanctuary in a remote village in the mountains of southern Shaanxi. The village, a single dirt road with a cluster of run-down houses, was too remote for people to find work, so that only children and the elderly remained. Utterly dispirited, they had largely given up hope and were just vegetating along.

When the Daoist arrived with his crew of builders and craftsmen, supported by state funds and city donors, they took notice. For the first time in years, someone looked at them as if they mattered. Their spirits rose and, as the temple started to look better, they began to renovate their houses. When it offered the first services to newly installed deities, they applied for government grants and paved the main road, constructed a community center, and began to take pride in their homes.

As the temple grew, moreover, tourists started to arrive, looking for peace and quiet as well as clean air and open nature. This fostered a whole new level of economic opportunity, leading to families offering B & B stays, local shops stacking more goods, and vendors selling religious paraphernalia. Adults now could make a living, and some of the migrant workers returned. The Daoist temple, in other words, not only rebuilt religious structures but gave the community a new lease on life, transforming it in the process.

YouTube: "Escaping from an Abandoned Chinese Temple"

Read: Wei, Yanli. 2017. "The Caishan Goddess Temple: Then and Now." *Journal of Daoist Studies* 10:196-210.

Liao, Yiwu. 2009. *The Corpse Walker: Real-Life Stories, China from the Bottom Up*. New York: Anchor, 73-92

25. Innovation and Consumption

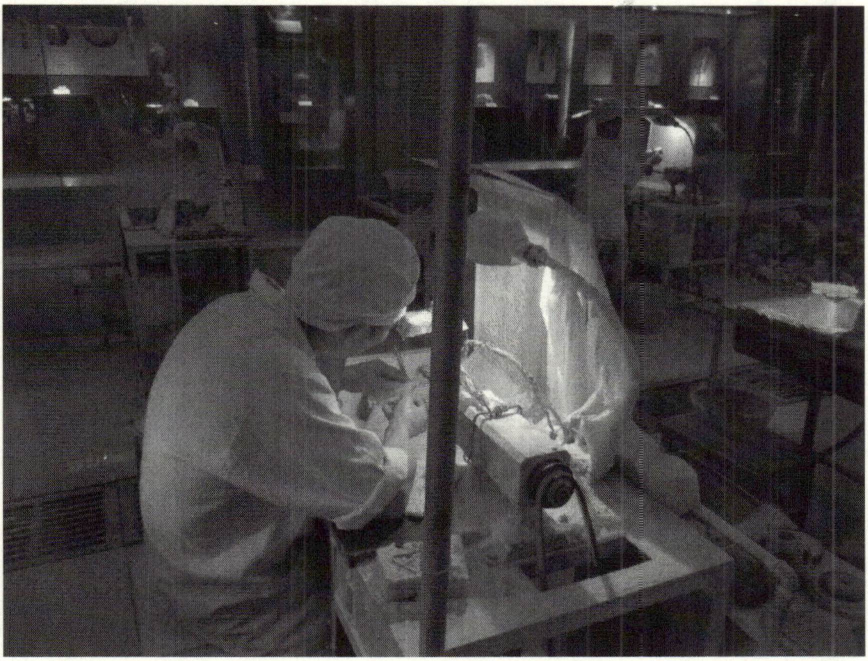

As the Chinese economy moves away from manufacturing and export, it is bound to slow, leading to predicted growth rates of 3-4 percent. If it is to keep up even that much momentum, it will need to shift toward new forms of commerce and business, toward technological innovation and creative solutions, as well as toward a massive increase in consumer spending.

Both are fraught with difficulties. Yes, there is bound to be an increase in consumer spending as the next hundreds of millions of people move up into the middle class, their incomes expected to rise by 15-20 percent annually. However, the Chinese traditionally have tended to be frugal and personal savings rates are high, 30 percent of income for those with full employment, up to 50 percent among migrant workers.

In today's China, this is mainly due to the lack of a reliable social network. There is no unemployment insurance, no pension scheme, no social security, no senior care, no assisted living, no hospice, and no fully reliably health care system. NGOs, which take care of many of these aspects in Western countries, and especially the U. S., are minimal and have to work semi-underground, since the government officially prohibits them in its drive toward total control. In other words, people save much of their disposable income to create a personal security net rather than increasing consumption.

Innovation, too, suffers from government control, especially internet and media censorship, hindering key axioms of science, such as skepticism, freedom of inquiry, respect for evidence, the equality of inquiring minds, and the universality of truth. Masking this, the state heavily invests in research, spending close to $50 billion annually, which is a lot in absolute terms but, according to the World Bank, makes up only about 2 percent of GDP, compared with 2.8 percent in the U.S., 3.5 in Japan, and 4.3 in South Korea.

In addition, the state directs where the money goes, particularly favoring large-scale engineering projects, such as transgenic crops, nuclear power, and lunar exploration. It tends to encourage quick successes and short-term gains that can show the Party in a positive light rather than ground-breaking new studies or long-term basic development. Being part of the government, moreover, research tends to suffer from bureaucratic oversight and a low work quality as well as from ubiquitous corruption. Some estimates suggest that as much as half of all allotted funds end up in private hands and do not actually support intended projects.

Private companies, in contrast, are more efficient and much more effective, leading to powerful instances of innovation that may yet slow considerably when the Social Credit System becomes mandatory. After all, why engage in experimental ventures and risk losing a good credit score when the tried and true guarantees success, at least for a while?

For now, though, there are a few areas where real innovation is happening. One is environmentally friendly construction, first models of which appeared in the wake of the Sichuan earthquake: using cheaper and more renewable materials, they produced easily assembled houses, well insulated, with built-in solar cells and power-saving devices.

A completely green or forest city that covers houses in greenery, relies on renewable energy, and uses non-polluting transportation, moreover, is under construction in Liuzhou, a town in the mountains of northern Guangxi. However, the idea is not Chinese, but rather relies on a design by the Italian architect Stefano Boeri (b. 1956), the creator of the "vertical forest," an ecological high-rise complex in Milan, and other similar projects.

Public transportation is another sore point for many Chinese. Thus, a company in Guangdong pioneered a fully self-driving streetcar system that runs on batteries fed by the friction of the rails, which themselves are not built into the tarmac but easily screwed on top.

Since going outside is becoming more of a hardship, given traffic density and pollution, many consumers are increasingly shopping online. In China, this also extends to groceries, a feature that never took off in the West and requires a whole new set of computer programming. In addition, they are now working on cell phone apps that track the provenance of each food item to its source to provide assurance about food safety. Another side effect is that delivery drivers and motor cycle riders are now among the best-paid low-skilled workers in the country.

The internet is yet another major area of innovation. Several key companies have made world=wide headlines for their strong innovative power. They include first of all Alibaba, the Chinese answer to Amazon, who developed an entirely new way of online payment processing that keeps customers free from the clutches of state-owned banks and avoids credit cards, which the debt-shy Chinese tend to eschew.

Then there is Xiaomi, a smartphone giant ironically called "Little Rice," who comes out with new ideas and app improvements every week, testing them live through immediate customer feedback, and thus creating systems that people really want.

Tencent, last but not least, is the largest online gaming company in the world. It also focuses on instant messaging, e-commerce, web browsers, and antivirus protection, and has been praised as the most innovative company on the planet.

Yet others include Apricot Forest with apps that help navigate the health care system; Baidu, the Chinese answer to Google, which provides increasingly efficient search engines, maps, and social media apps; Wanda, a real estate giant that also invests in public buildings like theaters, favoring unconventional forms of architecture; as well as a number of delivery companies that make online shopping more efficient, and more, new ventures to come.

YouTube: "Jack Ma Interview"

"China's Recent Major Achievements in Technology and Innovation"

Read: Shirky, Clay. 2015. *Little Rice: Smartphones, Xiaomi, and the Chinese Dream*. New York: Columbia Global Reports.

Tse, Edward. 2015. *China's Disruptors: How Alibaba, Xiaomi, Tencent, and Other Companies Are Changing the Rules of Business*. London: Portfolio Penguin.

26. Fairs and Festivals

While Daoist principles can make a contribution to innovative thinking, a topic discussed in Part Three below, it has a more hands-on impact on the economy in the area of consumption. Notably temple fairs and festivals offer great opportunities for people to engage in buying and selling, advance marketing and advertising.

Most inner-city temples have regular fairs. For example, the Baxian'an 八仙庵 (Eight Immortals' Hermitage) in the eastern part of downtown Xi'an holds a fair twice weekly, on Wednesdays and Sundays. A cross between a farmers' market and a flea market, it attracts vendors of all kinds and status, who spread throughout the neighborhood, especially to the south and east of the temple, while crowds throng the streets.

Offerings include fresh fruit and vegetables, clothes, household goods, pottery, knickknacks, religious paraphernalia, and antiques. Some vendors set up organized stalls on the roadside; others just spread a cloth to display their wares in squares and courtyards. In addition, shoppers can enjoy street food and snacks of all sorts and types, on-the-spot foot massages, and fortune-telling. The atmosphere is cheerful and vibrant, and a good time is had by all.

Festivals are fairs on steroids. They only occur once or twice a year, usually in conjunction with a major deity's birthday or at special seasonal occasions such as New Year's, but then they last several days or even a week. In addition to much larger numbers of vendors, coming from farther away and spreading more widely throughout the area, they come with elaborate rituals and performances of various kinds. Traditionally theater was always closely connected to religion, and many temples have stages for operatic and other presentations, dedicated primarily to the gods but also for humans to enjoy. In addition, festivals often feature daring acrobatics, magic shows, exploding fireworks, cacophonic music, lion dances, rhythmic drumming, as well as all different kinds of street performers and entertainers.

Beyond that, the local temple association will take the birthday god for a tour of the neighborhood, creating a noisy and colorful parade that may involve motorized vehicles, hand-drawn carts, people on foot, musical bands, and various special performers. Two groups of lay followers usually accompany the deities on foot, wearing a common uniform that consisting of T-shirts and ball caps bearing the name of the temple. One group usually has somewhat rough looking young men; the other—in sharp contrast—has merry older folks, both men and women. The former group can loosely be defined as temple parade security; the latter comprises the faithful who believe they gather divine favor by accompanying the parades.

All this creates great economic opportunity, businesses fulfilling the needs of active participants by supplying costumes, props, housing, and food, as well as catering to large crowds of onlookers and visitors, often from far away and in need of accommodation, sustenance, and souvenirs. Temples, thus, form a stage where people can engage in the age-old and today increasingly popular mix of religious devotion, tourism, and business.

YouTube: "China: Thousands Welcome the Year of the Rooster"

"Parade of Taiwanese Deities"

Read: Kennedy, Brian L, and Elizabeth Kuo. 2009. "Taiwanese Temple Parades and Their Martial Motifs." *Journal of Daoist Studies* 2:197-209.

Phillips, Scott Park. 2016. *Possible Origins: A Cultural History of Chinese Martial Arts, Theater, and Religion.* Boulder: Angry Baby Books.

27. Pilgrimages

Another form festivals take is pilgrimages to sacred sites to celebrate a particular deity on his or her holy day. They have played an important role in Chinese religion, documented from early ascents to sacred mountains to late medieval worship of the Perfect Warrior on Mount Wudang. After a hiatus during the Cultural Revolution, they have come to the fore again, to the point where in Beijing alone there are about eighty associations dedicated to celebrating the two-week festival of the Daoist Goddess of the Morning Clouds (Bixia yuanjun) at her sanctuary on Miaofeng shan 妙峰山, a medium-level peak about 40 miles west of the city.

These pilgrimage associations are non-profit organizations, encouraged and supervised by government officials, but essentially independent. They decide who gets to ascend the mountain and how they have to behave, what qualifications and requirements each has to meet. In all cases, the associations center on piety and charity. They come in two major forms, martial and civilian. While the former focus on physical performances, demonstrating their skills as lion dancers, sword fighters, stilt walkers, taiji boxers, acrobats, and more, the latter work to make the pilgrims welcome by providing them with physical and moral sustenance as they climb the mountain.

Each group dedicated to the Miaofeng shan event has about thirty to forty members; their founders often dedicated senior individuals, who either have a long family tradition of service or made a vow to give charity in this manner after the goddess helped them through a major crisis. Both apply to Ni Zhenshan, founder of the Whole Heart Philanthropic Salvation Tea Association, which runs a small shrine on the ascent to the sanctuary and there provides pilgrims with good-quality tea and steamed buns.

Chen Deqing, the founder of the Deqing Fresh Flower Association, began her activities in the 1980s, when, already in her fifties, she rode her pedal-powered trishaw to the mountain to honor the goddess with flowers. Today, with the support of family members and followers, she spends thousands of dollars on flowers while hosting her own shrine on the mountain and becoming a quasi-priestess for the festival's duration.

The pilgrimage to Miaofeng shan, as others around the country, has grown substantially over the years, and even members of the younger generation are increasingly participating. Thus, Ni Jintang, the younger son of the patriarch, eagerly stepped into a leadership role upon his father's passing, vigorously organizing the chaos of the first night, conscientiously recording the members' names, and generously offering donation opportunities to like-minded businessmen. Martial practitioners, too, engage more and more young people, who learn the arts of performance from their parents and grandparents while yet juggling busy lives in the city. Their repertoire may be smaller, their skills may not be as precisely honed, but the will is there, and the tradition continues.

YouTube: "2016 Miaofengshan Temple Fair"

Read: Johnson, Ian. 2017. *The Souls of China: The Return of Religion after Mao*. New York: Pantheon Books.

Lagerwey, John. 1992. "The Pilgrimage to Wu-tang Shan." In *Pilgrims and Sacred Sites in China*, edited by Susan Naquin and Chün-fang Yü, 293-332. Berkeley: University of California Press.

28. Major Life Events

Another area where Daoist traditions continue in a modern guise is the celebration of major life events, typically associated with what Arnold van Gennep (1909) has called "rites of passage." These are, most importantly, marriage, childbirth, and death—times when people pass from one social status to another, to being husband and wife, parents, and eventually ancestors. Lesser transitions of equal importance today are college graduation, the first job, and retirement, plus various other landmarks, such as promotions, opening a business, or a first home purchase.

In all these cases, people pass through a threshold or liminal phase, when they are no longer in one stage and have not yet reached the next. In other words, the bride going down the aisle is no longer a daughter and not yet a wife; the woman in labor is no longer pregnant and not yet a mother; the boy during initiation is no longer a child and not yet a man. This means that, in terms of social context, the person is for a time between positions assigned by law, custom, convention, and ceremony. Stripped of the values and symbols of ordinary society, he or she is reduced to a more basic level of being before being fashioned anew and endowed with the particular rights and duties the new rank.

All this requires spiritual and community assistance, as manifest worldwide in youth initiations (think bar mitzvah), weddings, college graduations, baptisms, funerals, and more. Typically, rites combine forms of thanksgiving with prayers for protection—for example, appreciating the divine support that led to the birth of the child in conjunction with invocations to keep it safe in life.

In China, unable to eliminate these festivities completely, the Party worked hard to strip them of their religious content and setting, replacing them with civil ceremonies while striving to put a stop to the—often devastating—expenses the ceremonies used to incur. Today, with modernization and prosperity being more commonplace, traditional celebrations have made a comeback, combined often also with increasingly fashionable Western forms, so that today brides often wear white and grooms show up in tuxedos.

Daoists as much as other religious specialists are actively involved in these various life events. They determine the most auspicious time and place for the ceremony, organize its parts according to five-phases cosmology, purify the ritual objects, invoke the proper deities, and send the correct petitions to the right divine officials. They also provide talismans for protection and set up divine support for the future. Besides the major transitions of life, they also perform blessings as needed, such as for a new house, a new car, a new job, overall ensuring that worldly life is connected to, and supported by, the greater cosmic realm.

YouTube: "How to Get Married in Ancient China"

Read: Saso, Michael. 1990. *Blue Dragon White Tiger: Taoist Rites of Passage*. Washington, D.C.: The Taoist Center.

Schmitz, Rob. 2016. *Street of Eternal Happiness: Big City Dreams along a Shanghai Road*. New York: Crown Publishers, ch. 12

Watson, James L., and Evelyn Rawski, eds. 1988. *Death Ritual in Late Imperial and Modern China*. Berkeley: University of California Press.

29. The Celestial Masters

While Daoist monastics of the Complete Perfection school, if assigned to city temples, will also perform relevant life ceremonies, most community Daoists are lay priests and belong to the school of the Celestial Masters (Tianshi 天师), more formally known as the Way of Orthodox Unity (Zhengyi dao 正一道).

The school was founded by the ecstatic seeker and alchemist Zhang Daoling after receiving a revelation in Sichuan, an event variously placed on either Mount Heming or Qingcheng. There, the story goes, in 142, Lord Lao appeared to him and told him that the end of the world was at hand. He was to instruct the people to repent and prepare themselves for the momentous changes by becoming morally pure, so that they could serve as the "seed people" of the new age of Great Peace (Taiping 太平). Closing the "Covenant of Orthodox Unity," the god appointed Zhang as his representative on earth with the title Celestial Master and gave him healing powers as a sign of his empowerment.

Zhang followed the god's orders and, in an era characterized by continuous disasters, gathered thousands of people around him. As a token for his efforts, he took five pecks of rice from his followers, whom he organized into tight units and controlled with a strict moral code and ritual schedule, creating a semi-independent state on a religious and ritual basis.

Seeing themselves as advisers rather than as an alternative to potent worldly rulers, the early Celestial Masters submitted to the warlord Cao Cao 曹操 around 215. In due course, he decided not to tolerate a separate organization in his territory and forcefully moved large numbers of Celestial Masters followers to different parts of the empire. There they spread their cult, merging with local and other Daoist traditions and transforming it gradually into a major organized religion that reached the entire country.

In the 12th century, moreover, their teaching was transmitted to the minority group of the Yao, who live in southwest China and northern Thailand. The practice has survived among them in particular purity, allowing a glimpse into its expression in history.

In China, too, the school is still active. The current Celestial Master, the 65th of his lineage, resides in Taiwan with mainland headquarters on Mount Longhu 龙虎山 in Jiangxi. Since the 1990s, they have made a major comeback here, especially in southeastern China. Their teaching focuses heavily on divine protection against demons, partly by receiving and carrying ritual registers with names of divine generals who can fight off all sorts of attacks. In addition, they provide relevant talismans, identify invading demons, and expel noxious influences with a variety of means—herbs, wands, chants, spells, dances, and more

Married and living in ordinary society, where they engage in various professions, Celestial Masters priests undergo a similar formal initiation as Complete Perfection followers, but then focus on managing a wide network of Daoist temples and communities. Often using rituals and methods transmitted in their families over many generations, they perform purifications, exorcisms, and cosmic renewal rituals.

YouTube: "Secret Magic behind a Fu Talisman"

Read: Alberts, Eli. 2006. *A History of Daoism and the Yao People of South China*. Youngtown, NY: Cambria Press.

Kleeman, Terry F. 2016. *Celestial Masters: History and Ritual in Early Daoist Communities*. Cambridge, Mass.: Harvard Yenching Institute.

Hsieh, Shu-Wei. 2016. "Possession and Ritual: Daoist and Popular Healing in Taiwan." *Journal of Daoist Studies* 9:73-100.

Yang, Fenggang. 2012. *Religion in China Today: Survival and Revival under Communist Rule*. New York: Oxford University Press.

30. Scams and Insecurities

A much less pleasant dimension of increased prosperity and economic freedom is the rise in fraudulent businesses and investment scams. China is full of both, some—such as the tinkering with baby formula—making worldwide headlines. Less well known are the actual numbers. For example, in 2014, financial scams conned people out of $24 billion, while more recently police arrested 21 people involved in a Ponzi scheme centered on Ezubao, the country's largest online financing platform, that netted them $7 billion.

Areas of fraud are widespread, including online marketing, metal works, agricultural products, streetcar systems, and more, usually with impressively documented assets that do not exist in actual fact. Rob Schmitz describes the situation vividly in his book, *Street of Eternal Happiness*. Friends with Auntie Fu, the wife of a pensioner who sells scallion pancakes out of his street-level window at 50 cents a pop, he does his best to dissuade her from investing in questionable schemes.

These involve a mushroom farm in the northeast without any mushrooms, a mall-centered sales scheme focusing on special-app terminals, and others of similar ilk. Dead set on making a killer in the market, deluded by entirely fictional profit figures—especially in contrast to the interest rates offered by banks—and impressed by the claim that the companies are listed on Western stock exchanges, Auntie Fu remains undeterred and loses close to $50,000 of her hard-earned pension.

Many Chinese are in the same boat, as protests in various places document, but they are not alone. Over seventy Chinese companies, listed at the New York Stock Exchange, were found fraudulent and banned, but only after numerous Americans made substantial investments in them.

Daoism, too, is not exempt from this trend, as the well-publicized case of Li Yi 李一 (b. 1969) documents, a master "not of the constant way," as the magazine headline puts it. An initiated Daoist master, Li Yi served as abbot of the Shaolong guan 绍龙观 (Summoning Dragons Temple), located in the Jinyun shan 缙云山 nature preserve near the mega-city of Chongqing in southwest China.

Claiming to have started Daoist practice at age 3 and attained academic recognition by major universities—both entirely fictional—he styled himself a living god in possession of supernatural healing powers. To prove these, he regularly faked miracles and soon attracted over 60,000 followers, including some well-known pop stars and internet giants like Jack Ma. In the process, he made himself rich by charging thousands of dollars for spa treatments and courses in magical powers.

Coming to the attention of the authorities, the Bureau of Religious Affairs started an investigation into his claims and practices in 2010, leading to a formal trial and sentencing to several years in prison. The case has highlighted the potential dangers of miracle healers and thrown a rather unfavorably light on the local Daoist Association, which allowed him not only to practice unchallenged but also supported his rise to the status of abbot within its ranks.

YouTube: "Thousands Protest over Investment Scams in Anyang, China"

"Feds: China Won't Help Stop Investment Scams"

Read: Schmitz, Rob. 2016. *Street of Eternal Happiness: Big City Dreams along a Shanghai Road*. New York: Crown Publishers, chs. 9, 11.

31. Fortune-Telling

One way to counteract the potential scams and frauds, as well as get a handle on other sources of insecurity, where honest Daoists are of great help, is the traditional art of fortune-telling. This comes in two major forms, temple oracles and personal consultation.

Temple oracles involve invocation of the deity by bowing before him or her, offering a prayer that contains the question to be asked, then picking a numbered wooden stick from a round bamboo container and verifying the accuracy of this choice by throwing half-moon shaped yin-yang blocks that are flat on one side and round on the other. If they land one up, one down, the god approves of the stick chosen; if not, one has to pray and pick again. Having ascertained the number, one goes to the temple office right there in or next to the sanctuary and obtains a "fortune slip," a small strip of paper that contains a poem as well as some specific information, detailing one's fortune.

Personal consultation is more in-depth, more long-term, and more detailed, and can best be described as fate calculation (*suanming* 算命). It typically works with the eight characters—the traditional way of naming one's year, month, day, and hour of birth—and provides information both on overall destiny, i. e., major changes that occur in the course of several decades, and more specific short-term tendencies for the next few years.

Many Daoists practice this art. As Adeline Herrou shows in her study of Wengongci monk Yang Zhixiang as well as in her video about Master Feng, they are rather careful about it, too. "In fate," Yang says, "there is the part on which one can act (temporary fortune) and another about which nothing can be done (overall destiny). Even then, some fortune remains impervious to all attempts of change." Despite this, people always have free will and make choices: they have to take responsibility for how they conduct their lives. It is part of the Daoists' skill that they present the inherent tendencies they see without limiting the individual's power, while yet preparing their clients for developments they cannot control.

A prime area of fate calculation is the selection of a marriage partner, which has become more complicated in modernity as traditional family structures disintegrate and match-makers are far and few between. Still considered the joining of two families rather than two individuals, it is fraught with anxiety, and parents often advertise their children, complete with pictures and personal information, in a public marriage market, held in a city park either on their own initiative or through a dating service. The Chinese equivalent of personal newspaper ads and online dating, this is yet completely different in that the parents are the main movers, and the children may not even know this is happening.

An interview with a Daoist priest to check the compatibility of fate according to the eight characters would happen long after this advertising stage, today ranking after education, income, and home ownership.

YouTube: "Traditional Chinese Fortune Telling"

"An Idiot Abroad: China—Fortune Teller"

Read: Herrou, Adeline. 2010. "A Day in the Life of a Daoist Monk." *Journal of Daoist Studies* 3:117-48.

Morgan, Carole. 1998. "Old Wine in a New Bottle: A New Set of Oracle Slips from China." *Journal of Chinese Religions* 26: 1-20.

32. Pollution

Some parents might be glad their children are not marrying and having offspring of their own, given the dreadful rate of pollution in China. For example, the so-called Airpocalypse Beijing in 2013 saw air quality above 700 on the Air Quality Index (AQI). This measures especially PM 2.5 particles, chemical units so small that they get past most nostril filters and penetrate the lungs. This rating is over 30 times worse than WHO recommended levels. To compare, Singapore in the same year declared an emergency at 300 AQI reading. Los Angeles, America's most polluted city, usually tops off at around 100, and Paris declared a state of emergency in March 2014 when the AQI hit 150, banning half the city's cars from the road.

Concerns over pollution are one of the top-five fears of consumers in China. People with resources relocate overseas, wanting to raise their children in a healthy environment. On the other end of the scale, foreign companies cannot get executives to live in country; if they have to work there, they commute while their families stay home. Ordinary people wear face masks, available in increasingly creative and fashionable designs, and order as much as they can online. They also voice protests with increasing frequency, being more aware of just how bad it is, since cell phones and internet connections record AQI ratings in real time.

Already a quarter million people die every year prematurely due to pollution, and 40 percent of all deaths can be linked to it—in addition to increasingly fatty diets (China is now the second most obese nation after America).

One major driving force behind pollution is car ownership, up from 6.5 million drivers in 2003 to 85 million in 2013. Exhaust from cars makes up about 30 percent of China's pollution. Already all motor cycles are electric, and the government strongly favors battery-driven vehicles. It is set to implement steadily increasing quotas that reward oil-free engines, in conjunction with ever improving public transportation, hoping to eliminate this source of pollution over the next decade or two.

Another, even stronger source of pollution is power made from coal, which supplies 70 percent of all Chinese energy needs. Again, the government is well aware of the situation and worried about growing unrest. It is shutting down many smaller and older plants and systematically supports renewable sources of energy. However, it also plans to build more, newer, and bigger coal plants. These are slated to increase the pollution level even more for at least another decade.

In addition, water ways are polluted, lakes full of algae fish dying in rivers, and ponds vanishing. What used to be scenic spots by rivers or lakes are now algae-infested and garbage-strewn wastelands. Ground water, too, is not exempt from this trend, pollution greatly impacting its quality

Another issue is water supply, especially in the north which receives relative little rain fall. This is somewhat alleviated by the so-called South-to-North Water Diverion Project, a mega infrastructure investment similar to the Three Gorges Dam on the Yangtze. Eventually it will channel 44.8 billion cubic meters of fresh water annually from southern rivers to the thirsty north, using three canal systems along the Grand Canal; the Han River, and a western line across and through mountains. Some routes are already operational, and Beijing receives 70 percent of its water from the south. Still, the overall water level of the country is sinking, and one prediction has China running out of water by 2030.

YouTube: "China's Toxic Smog"

"20 Signs China's Pollution Has Reached Apocalyptic Levels"

Read: Martin, Richard. 2015. *Coal Wars: The Future of Energy and the Fate of the Planet.* New York: Palgrave Macmillan.

Minter, Adam. 2013. *Junkyard Planet: Travels in the Billion-Dollar Trash Trade.* New York: Bloomsbury.

Rein, Shaun. 2014. *The End of Copycat China: The Rise of Creativity, Innovation, and Individualism in Asia.* New York: Wiley.

33. Daoist Resorts

Besides invoking Daoist ideas of honoring nature and protecting the environment (see # 50 below), monastics have begun to style their mountain and country temples as pollution sanctuaries and are increasingly reinventing themselves as environmentalists.

Mountains are by nature away from cities and industrial zones, plus they tend to rise up into the skies, often reaching above toxic vapors. When I first climbed Huashan in 1991, I was surprised to see real sunlight once I got to a certain level, something entirely absent in the plains and cities below. In addition, the notion of "sacred mountain" encourages a strong sense of protection, not only for humans but also for animals and trees, supporting biodiversity and seeing all as part of an integrated universal and cosmic system that should not be tinkered with.

To enhance the purity of their centers, as Yang Shihua, abbot of Maoshan, the center of the Highest Clarity school, notes, Daoists erect their structures in an environmentally friendly manner, building around existing trees and rock formations. They use renewal solar energy rather than coal-produced electricity, keep motorized traffic to a minimum, conserve and recycle all materials as much as possible, and in general create a wholesome and healthy environment while encouraging greater ecological awareness.

In addition, and with full support of the Chinese Daoist Association, they also offer resort-type spa services, often invoking the Daoist ideal of longevity. An example I visited a few years ago is the Daoist Long Life Center in the Blue Iris Garden (Qingzhi yuan 青芷园) condo complex in Beijing. Run by Wang Chengya 王称雅, a Peking University graduate and White Cloud ordinand, the Center at the time occupied several floors of the community building. Arranged according to fengshui principles, its rooms are extremely well furnished and tastefully decorated with Daoist art.

Clients are first taken to two intake rooms to have themselves evaluated for physical ailments and astrological predispositions. They then receive a treatment plan, which includes dietary suggestions, herbal concoctions, special teas as well as herbal baths, massages, facials, qigong, and healing exercises. The Center employs an extensive staff and has a high rate of success, treating senior party cadres, the prime minister, and increasing numbers of foreigners.

Its model has been replicated widely among Daoist centers and especially mountains, where healthy living is a growing focus—entirely in line with the traditional Daoist view that all spiritual development begins with a healthy body, where *qi* flows smoothly and harmoniously. Also in line with historical precedent is the notion of temples as resorts—documented as far back as the Tang dynasty 1200 years ago and well described for the early 20th century, city dwellers would relocate to the mountains in the summer to escape the heat and humidity, then use the opportunity to improve their health and learn various longevity techniques—from diet through herbs, teas, exercise, and breathing to deep levels of meditation.

YouTube: "Taoist Monks Find New Role as Environmentalists"

"China: Religion and Environment"

Read: Goullart, Peter. 1961. *The Monastery of Jade Mountain*. London: John Murray.

34. Nutrition

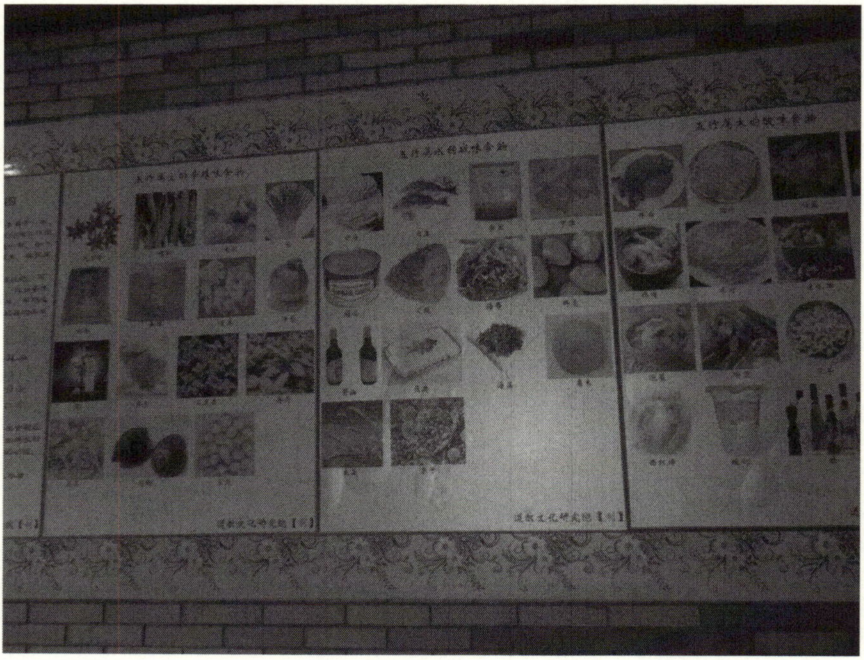

Going beyond mountain resorts, Daoist dietetics are having an increased impact on Chinese society, especially since questions of nutrition and food safety are becoming ever more important.

Westernization and advanced technology, while increasing food production and encouraging a more lavish lifestyle, also brought the tendency to alter and denature foodstuffs. The most blatant examples include the polishing of rice and bleaching of wheat flour, which began in China in the late 19th century. Similarly, modern bio-engineering often reduces the nutritional value of basic staples and encourages the consumption of empty calories, leading to new and increased health problems, such as hypertension, diabetes, and obesity.

Not immune to these development, the Chinese have altered their eating habits, consuming fewer fruits and vegetables and more items containing fat, flour, and sugar: soft drinks, candy, cookies, hamburgers, and the like. This situation is exacerbated by issues of food safety, compromised not only due to pollution, pesticides, and antibiotics, but often caused intentionally by unscrupulous manipulators. A prime example is the 2008 melamine scandal, when tainted baby food harmed and even killed infants. As a result, people today are highly concerned about where their food is coming from, and more and more consumers insist on organic production.

Traditional Daoist dietetics, with their high respect for nature and a profound awareness of the impact different foods have on the energy system of the body, can make an important contribution to healthy living. Not only do Daoists rely dominantly on vegetables—monastics eating vegetarian—but they also emphasize purity in preparation and utensils, avoid overly stimulating and heating foods, such as onions, garlic, and ginger, and match food choice and intake to seasonal change.

Rather than based on content such as carbohydrates and protein, they classify foods by energetic impact. Thus, yang foods are stimulating, warming, and *qi*-enhancing, e. g., apricots, barley, cherries, pineapple, plums, celery, and coconut. Yin foods are calming, cooling and *qi*-settling>. Examples are bananas, tofu, cucumbers, eggplant, lettuce, mushrooms, pumpkins, tomatoes, and watermelon. Neutral foods are neither yin nor yang but generally *qi*-maintaining; here we have apples, cabbage, carrots, papaya, grain, beans, and eggs.

These properties, moreover, are associated with the four seasons, with people's ages, and with particular mental states. Thus, foods eaten in spring should be stimulating and neutral; in summer, they should have a calming and cooling effect. By the same token, young people tend to be warmer, more energetic, and more yang in quality, needing calming and cooling foods, while older folks have increased yin and tend to like meats, stews, and warming dishes. A lack of confidence, moreover, can be alleviated by consuming more yang food, while tendencies toward aggression will benefit from a mellowing yin-rich diet.

Organic, vegetarian restaurants that take these aspects into consideration are multiplying and becoming widely popular today, often run by Buddhists but increasingly also by Daoists. In addition, some Daoists run restaurants specializing in medicated dishes (*yaoshan* 藥膳) that bolster and tonify *qi* as part of nutritional therapy or personal self-care. These dishes, geared to individual conditions, balance yin and yang, prevent and treat diseases, strengthen the constitution, and lengthen life. Many restaurants cater particularly to middle-aged men, helping them to supplement *qi*, prevent the depletion of sexual essence, and generally improve the functioning of the inner organs. Dishes include regular foodstuffs, supplemented by *qi*-enhancing herbs, such as ginseng, astralagus, schisandra, chrysanthemum, fennel, hawthorn, and Asian cornelian cherry, all part and parcel of the Daoist apothecary.

YouTube: "China's Tough New Food Safety Law Takes Effect"

"Vegetarian Buddhist Cuisine"

Read: Anderson, Eugene N., and Marja L. Anderson. 1977. "Modern China: South." In *Food in Chinese Culture*, edited by K. C. Chang, 317-82. New Haven: Yale University Press.

Kohn, Livia. 2010. *Daoist Dietetics: Food for Immortality*. Dunedin, Fla.: Three Pines Press.

35. Health Care

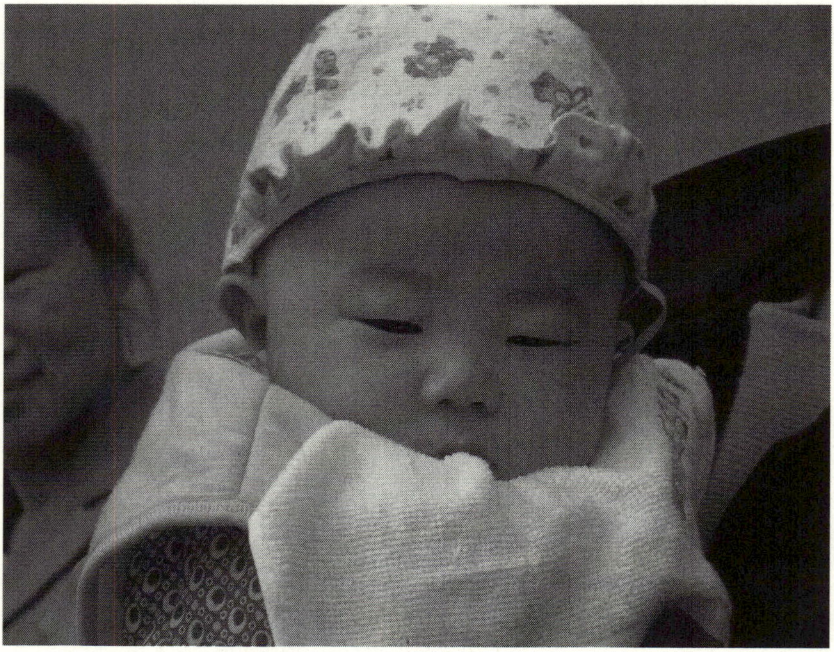

Energy-enhancing eating and a healthy lifestyle as taught in Daoist resorts are becoming ever more important, given the problematic state of China's health care system. While everyone received free care under Mao, economic development reduced state involvement to the point that, by 2003, only about 30 percent of the population had basic health care.

This number has grown considerably over the years, so that today most Chinese are covered, mainly due to the new rural cooperative medical care initiative. A voluntary system, funded by individual contributions and government subsidies, it reaches wide swathes of the population, although it continues to be plagued by inadequate funding, staff shortages, and insufficient equipment.

One issue is that while inpatient costs are covered, most outpatient visits are not, which leaves many people still unable to pay. Also, location matters, again referring back to the ubiquitous household registration system. Rural medical care covers 70-80 percent of a visit to the local clinic, but only about 60 at the county hospital, and even less for more specialist services, often located in bigger cities. Migrant workers again fall through the cracks, having no access to state-run health services where they live.

In addition, waiting times are long, often lasting hours One can pay especially to get a prebooked time slot or hire someone to stand in line in one's stead, but both cost money. Also, physicians are notoriously underpaid and overworked, commonly making less than $800 a month, even in larger cities. One brain surgeon in Tianjin, as Shaun Rein points out, made so little he had to take bribes just to cover his basic living expenses.

Given this situation, doctors often require a "red envelope" filled with private cash to do a proper job. They also tend to overprescribe medicines for percentages from the pharmaceutical industry and recommend unnecessary surgeries to get kickbacks. Typically, they have little time or consideration for patients who they see in rooms filled with dozens of people, affording essentially no privacy or opportunity for calm and quiet conversation.

As a result, lower-income consumers feel helpless and angry at the medical system. "Poor people," Shaun Rein quotes an informant, "in China cannot afford to get sick. We have no insurance and do not trust doctors" (2014, 57). Protests are on the rise. In 2012, for example, the Chinese Hospital Association found that on average each hospital in China had 27.3 violent incidents, up from an average of 20.6 in 2008, bur rising to a total of over 20,000 in the country in 2013. Some of these protests even turn violent. For example, a patient in Harbin stabbed four hospital workers, killing one, because he did not receive appropriate attention.

Responding to these protests, the government has cracked down on corruption, notably abuses of medical funds but also on bribes taken by physicians and administrators. In addition, it has started a new campaign, Healthy China 2020. By this date, all citizens should have access to high-quality health care while living healthier lives overall. Focusing on urban areas most impacted by Westernization, the state encourages people to eat a more traditional diet and get more exercise—although with pollution on the rise the latter is a double-edged sword.

YouTube: "China's Ailing Healhcare System"

Read: Burns, Lawton Robert, and Gordon G. Liu, eds. 2017. *China's Health Care System and Reform.* Cambridge: Cambridge University Press

Rein, Shaun. 2014. *The End of Copycat China: The Rise of Creativity, Innovation, and Individualism in Asia.* New York: Wiley.

36. Temple Clinics

Corruption and uncaring physicians occur mainly in hospitals practicing Western biomedicine. Traditional Chinese doctors, who use various indigenous methods such as herbs, massages, cupping, acupuncture, and dietary modification, by the nature of their field have to look at the whole patient, including his social situation, lifestyle, and mental attitude. Despite serious Communist efforts to modernize and streamline these methods into a biomedically acceptable system with streamlined treatment protocols, formally known as TCM, doctors still see symptoms as indications of systemic imbalance and prescribe lifestyle changes as much as interventions by herbs or needles.

Daoists, never entirely taken in by TCM, follow a system called Classical Chinese Medicine that adheres strictly to the ancient teachings as codified in the *Huangdi neijing* 黄帝内经 (Inner Classic of the Yellow Emperor) and specially geared toward individual uniqueness and personal cultivation. Seeing the body as a major portal to spiritual cultivation, Daoists have long had an intimate connection to medicine. Many leading Daoists were also physicians, and vice versa—the most prominent being Sun Simiao 孙思邈 (581-682), Tang dynasty Daoist, alchemist, physician, pharmacologist, and more, now widely venerated as the King of Medicines (Yaowang 药王).

Today, many temples house clinics, and monks often train in medicine. Thus, for example, Huang Zongsheng 黄宗胜, abbot of the Changchun guan 长春观 (Temple of Eternal Spring) in Wuhan, specialized in herbal formulas, notably for swollen eyes and female troubles. He not only prices his medicines low, so people can afford them, but also offers them in free trials, not charging anything at all until patients experience some relief. In addition, he and other Daoist doctors often hold free clinics for the poor, working the first half of the day for free, then seeing paying patients in the afternoon. Part of their service to society and world, this is possible because the temple takes care of their room and board, and they have few personal needs and no dependents to support.

Generally, temple clinics use the full gamut of Chinese medical techniques to treat and strive to create a something they call "Daoism in life" (*shenghuo daojiao* 生活道教). This vision encourages temple Daoists to offer social in addition to medical services, such as psychological counseling for people confused by the modern world, thereby raising the religion's presence in society.

Another form of Daoist health care is *qi*-healing, using vital energy to stimulate physical health, either activated by the patient through qigong exercises or infused by a practitioner via laying-on of hands. While qigong as an unsupervised, private community practice has been outlawed since the Falungong protests in 1999, its medical use in properly accredited and government-supported clinics has been on the rise.

One example is the Eight Trigrams Red Cross Medical Exchange Center in the western outskirts of Beijing. Founded by Master Wan Sujian (b. 1953), originally a Western-style physician who worked for the People's Liberation Army, it offers training in qigong exercises, vigorous (almost acrobatic) gongfu routines, external *qi*-healing, traditional music, tea ceremony, and Daoist ritual.

While exercises tonify the elixir fields, purify the meridians, strengthen vital essence, and harmonize yin and yang, external *qi*-healing involves both hands-on massage techniques and external *qi* transmission without direct touch. These and other forms of energy treatments closely engage the patient in the healing process, gradually shifting both diagnostic awareness and control over treatment protocols to the patient.

YouTube: "Chinese Medicine—An Ancient Practice"

Read: Liu, Xun. 2008. "Profile of a Quanzhen Doctor: Abbot Huang Zongsheng at Wuhan's Monastery of Eternal Spring." *Journal of Daoist Studies* 1:145-60.

Rinaldini, Michael. 2008. "How I Became a Daoist Priest." *Journal of Daoist Studies* 1:181-87.

Favraud, Georges. 2016. "Immortals' Medicine: Daoist Healers and Social Change." *Journal of Daoist Studies* 9:101-20.

37. Qigong

The most radical empowerment of individuals with regard to health in China today is the practice of qigong 气功 or "energy work," a system of slow body movements in coordination with deep breathing and mental guiding of *qi* that releases tension, effects healing, and contributes to overall well-being. It began in 1947, when a leading cadre named Liu Guizhen 刘贵真 fell terminally ill and recovered with the help of traditional Daoist exercises. The Party, seeing the potential for widespread health care, adopted them in its own way, coining the new term "qigong" and making sure that the practice would be free from ancient cosmological concepts and superstitions while becoming more compatible with Western science.

Organized first in the 1950s, qigong served as the main vehicle of health maintenance for Party cadres. Limited to healing purposes, it was practiced solely in a medical setting, notably in specialized clinics in the scenic mountains north of Beijing. The practice made few inroads among the larger populace, and any research and publications served to make it less traditional and more scientific. This phase ended in the mid-1960s with the Cultural Revolution, when qigong was banned and practitioners went underground.

The 1970s saw the emergence of large-scale qigong self-healing by ordinary people—the kind of practice most closely associated with the term in the West. This new mode was particularly inspired by Guo Lin, a Beijing actress and daughter of Party cadres, who had used the techniques to cure herself of uterine cancer in the 1960s. When she suffered a relapse, she made the methods public and began to teach them to cancer patients in parks. She persisted in the face of police harassment and occasional imprisonment, frequently moving parks while increasing her following. By 1975, her methods had become well known and began to receive the support of Party cadres. Others imitated her style and, after the end of the Cultural Revolution and Mao's death in 1976, numerous practitioners "came out the mountains."

As they engaged in teaching, publications, and healing sessions, the people enthusiastically embraced the practices and followers came to number in the millions. They experienced qigong as a welcome relief after the forced communal activities and intense persecutions of the Cultural Revolution. Instead of being pushed about and having to engage in various campaigns, people could now voluntarily congregate and work on their bodies in a sphere that remained largely free of Party supervision.

This changed in the 1980s, when the government began to set up various national and regional organizations, sort of the Daoist Association for qigong, to monitor and control the practice. At the same time, its main popular focus shifted away from healing to the acquisition of extraordinary powers like clairvoyance, telepathy, psychokinesis, distance healing, and so on. The craze for these powers slowed down in the 1990s, when several highly popular masters were arrested for fraud and many feats were unveiled as quackery.

While the state issued more stringent regulations, demanding that qigong leaders be certified doctors or therapists, millions of followers found themselves at a loss of who to trust. This vacuum was filled by new groups that made ethics a fundamental part of the practice and added more religious features, such as chanting, ritual, and meditation. To all intents and purposes new religions, they claimed to lead their followers to transcendent salvation. Typical groups at the time were Zangmigong 藏秘功 (Tantric Qigong), for all intents and purposes a new form of Tibetan Buddhism, and Zhonggong 中功 (Central Qigong), an extensive organization that led practitioners to ultimate liberation through eight levels of increasingly religious practices.

The most prominent among them, with millions of followers, was Falungong 法轮功 (www.falundafa.org), a messianic cult founded in 1992 by Li Hongzhi 李洪志. A self-proclaimed bodhisattva, he set out to rid the planet of demons and ready it for the new world to come. To this end, he controlled people's lives and minds, prohibiting the reading of anything except his books and any healing methods besides his five key practices. He was also opposed to mixed marriages, women's autonomy, and various other modern features. His group was outlawed in 1996 and has been actively persecuted since 1999. Even today, as Liao Yiwu documents, some people are still hiding from the authorities, living without proper registration and in constant fear.

The fall-out from the persecution was that all modern forms of qigong—unlike ancient healing exercises—are now technically prohibited in China and should not be practiced in public. Exercise in parks today tends to focus on taiji quan (officially sanctioned as a sport with Olympic aspirations), Western-style aerobics, ballroom dancing, as well as various new forms of movement to music. Also, yoga is making great headway in China, seen entirely as a physical workout to the exclusion of all spirituality or religious context.

At the same time, Daoist temples, adapting to the physical fitness market, sponsor exercise practice closely matching qigong patterns for lay followers and encourage it among its residents. Some of them have also developed specific styles so that, in addition to Wudang martial arts, there are now systems related to various holy places, such as the Mount Emei Sage Style in 24 movements that opens the meridians and enhances internal healing.

An example that shows just how much Daoists have adopted bodily well-being as part of their doctrine appears in the short pamphlet *Daojiao yangsheng quanxiao geyan* 道教养生全孝格言 (Pertinent Words on Daoist Long Life and Filial Piety), a publication of the sanctuary on top of Mount Qingcheng. Entirely focused on health, it encourages physical movement along the lines of qigong without ever mentioning the term.

> Practice self-massage.
> Study fist or sword,
> Kick a ball,
> Or go for a walk,
> Maybe bathe in sunlight—
> But never cease your efforts.

Its only more religious note is an encouragement to "accumulate merit" by doing good deeds and behaving ethically, which too will aid health and long life by keeping the conscience clean and the mind pure.

YouTube: "Qigong—China"

Read: Palmer, David. 2007. *Qigong Fever: Body, Science and Utopia in China*. New York: Columbia University Press.

Kohn, Livia. 2008. *Chinese Healing Exercises: The Tradition of Daoyin*. Honolulu: University of Hawai'i Press.

Liao, Yiwu. 2009. *The Corpse Walker: Real-Life Stories, China from the Bottom Up*. New York: Anchor, 230-41.

38. Auspicious Graves

Even with all the qigong and mental purity, life eventually comes to an end. As traditional belief has it, human beings consist of two parts that in themselves contain both physical and spiritual elements, that is, slower and faster oscillations of *qi*.

These parts are a heavenly or more spiritual (yang) dimension, the so-called spirit soul (*hun* 魂), which comes from heaven; and an earthly and more material (yin) part, known as the material soul (*po* 魄), which arises from earth. They come together during gestation and are fully viable throughout life, guiding people toward more spiritual, artistic, and intellectual pursuits (*hun*)while also making sure they remain alive by providing instinctual needs for food, sleep, and companionship (*po*).

At death, the two separate and go back to their realms of origin. Thus, the spirit soul, guided in a formal funeral, moves up to reside in an ancestral heaven. Its symbolic replica on earth is the ancestral tablet, today often complete with a photograph of the deceased, through which it is honored and spiritually fed. Traditionally kept on the ancestral altar in the family home, it is today mostly placed in a pagoda at a Buddhist (and to a lesser degree Daoist) temple, where it receives regular blessings through the monks' chanting.

The material soul stays with the physical corpse of the person, whose remains—today usually cremains—are buried in a cemetery. Traditionally, it required grave goods, including meals, gifts, texts, and personal belongings. Today, these are still provided at funerals, consisting mostly of paper replicas of desirable items. Ancestors are believed to be conscious and knowledgeable of their descendants' affairs. They require regular supplies of food, wine, incense, and incantations, and will in due return send good fortune and provide protection. The relationship is strictly reciprocal, and disasters and illnesses in life are often attributed to neglect of one's ancestral duties.

Ghosts in this context are unhappy or discontented dead. Some are people who died violently coming back to wreak vengeance; others are ancestors who have been neglected by their families and badly in need of sustenance; yet others are mutant animals, creatures that have somehow gained the power to change their shape and cause trouble. To deal with these, people take basic precautions such as hanging demon-dispelling branches or talismans over their doors, muttering spells against ghosts whenever they enter an unknown area, or performing a divination before venturing out. In some cases, a community decides to take on the proper worship of such an entity, and a ghost can develop into a god, especially if prayers or rites turn out to be highly efficacious.

A key factor in the after-death process is the siting of graves, matching the belief, still important today, that ancestral spirits only rest properly and benefit the living if their material souls are in proper harmony with the earth. Using methods of fengshui, learned masters who are often Daoists calculate the best place and time of interment. Both have to match the birth and death dates of the deceased, and especially the exact direction and layout of the grave has a direct and inescapable influence on the good fortune of the surviving family.

Picking up on old customs, wealthier people today, as Liao Yiwu describes in his interview with Huang Tianyuan, a 90-year-old fengshui master, pick and develop auspicious spots for their own graves while still alive. One leading local official, he relates, purchased the indicated spot, had a major tomb structure erected, and moved all his ancestors into it. "He also ordered the craftsmen to build a grave for himself, which was more spacious than his house. After the project was completed, the chief hosted a huge banquet, with twenty tables full of guests." This lavishness, however, was counterproductive to the fengshui master. "I was invited but didn't go. I got my butt out of there as soon as I could. If a person becomes too greedy, he starts to carry bad energy. I was afraid he would pass that bad energy on to me."

YouTube: "Complete Guide to Prosperity Live Burial"

Read: Liao, Yiwu. 2009. *The Corpse Walker: Real-Life Stories, China from the Bottom Up*. New York: Anchor, 61-72.

39. The Li Priests

A group of priests specializing in Daoist rituals, notably funerals, are the members of the Li family from Yanggao 陽高 county in Shanxi, one of several local ensembles. Lay practitioners who have transmitted their art over many generations, they call themselves "yin-yang" to indicate that they traverse the worlds of the living and the dead.

The current patriarch is Li Manshan 李滿山 (b. 1946), a versatile musician and experienced ritual specialist who stays close to his native village and pays little attention to material possessions. He learned his skills from his father Li Qing 李清 (1926-1999), an awesome player of the mouth-organ as well as an impressive master of ritual and vocal liturgy. The next generation is led by Li Manshan's son Li Bin 李斌 (b. 1977), who moved to the county seat so that his young son could get a better education and is expanding the group's clientele to city dwellers.

Their main skills involve fortune-telling, scripture recitation, and music—the latter being what catapulted them into national and international recognition, giving performances at Carnegie Hall and all over Europe. Locally they serve after a death has occurred. First, they site the grave using a fengshui compass and determine the most auspicious time of burial with the help of the deceased's eight characters.

Then they hand-paint the coffin with efficacious talismans, usually on the third day after the death, a process that may take up to seven hours. Before the actual funeral, they decorate the soul hall, commonly the living room of the deceased's home, and provide the paper artifacts that will accompany him to heaven: houses, cars, feasts, money, and more. Li Bin and his wife make these paper replicas in their funerary shop in town, while back in the village Li Manshan's wife helps out with sundry tasks (see https://stephenjones.blog/the-film/).

At the actual funeral, which lasts several days, they dress up in formal Daoist gear, complete with mortarboard hats, to play numerous tunes, commonly lasting from 15 to 30 minutes each and often accompanied by the chanting of relevant scriptures. They do this throughout the entire liturgy, from Announcement through Opening Scriptures, Thanking the Earth, Inviting Deities, and Transferring Offerings all the way to Burial. On occasion, Li Manshan writes out magical symbols on red strips of paper used to seal the coffin. In between bouts of music, the Daoists rest and connect to the community.

Li Manshan's band consists of six players, mostly family members but also including Wu Mei 吳美, who as a teenager found himself fascinated by the profession and asked to become Li Qing's disciple. He is now the group's star player, a virtuoso on any instrument who often plays solos. Instruments include different kinds of drums, gongs, cymbals, conches, clarinets, mouth-organs, and strings. The tunes, often discordant and haunting, convey messages to the divine, including the announcement of the death, the desire for deliverance into an immortals' heaven, and blessings for the descendants.

For national and international performances, the ensemble chooses an adapted program, beginning with an opening procession around the hall onto the stage, using mouth-organ rather than the traditional percussion for Opening Scriptures. Feeling that the mournful cadences of the initial piece that lasts seventeen minutes may be too heavy for the uninitiated, they just sing the first three couplets. Next comes an abbreviated version of a long mouth-organ suite, followed by the uproarious Catching the Tiger sequence. Yellow Dragon Thrice Transforms Its Body, finale of the Transferring Offerings ritual, makes a rousing percussion interlude, and they conclude with a rather short version of a medieval hymn, leading into the final Chasing Round the Five Quarters.

YouTube: "Li Manshan: Protrait of a Folk Daoist"

"Folk Daoist Ritual Music"

Read: Jones, Stephen. 2010. *In Search of the Folk Daoists in North China* Farnham, UK: Ashgate Publications.

Jones, Stephen. 2017. *Daoist Priests of the Li Family: Ritual Life in Rural China*. St. Petersburg, Fla.: Three Pines Press.

40. Underground Churches

A yet different facet of the Chinese religious scene is underground or house churches, spiritual organizations not officially registered with the state that yet attract large numbers of followers. The Bureau of Religious Affairs not only requires formal and detailed registration, comparable to applying for non-profit status in a Western country, but it also imposes various rules and regulations, including political and doctrinal guidelines that impact organizational structure and might change the fundamental tenets of the groups' direction.

As a result, many opt to operate outside of official parameters, which makes them underground but not secret, active but not incorporated. Rather than hiding them from the official eye, it puts them on the list of suspicious organizations, prevents them from buying land or build a proper church, and alerts the security police, who routinely come by to request a list of members, park conspicuously in the neighborhood, and otherwise make their presence known.

Most underground churches are Christian, serving about half of China's 100 million believers. An example is the Early Rain Reformed Church in Chengdu (Chengdu qiuyu zhi fujiaohui 成都秋雨之福教会) under the leadership of Wang Yi 王怡 (b. 1973), a former civil rights lawyer. Renting a space in a modern high-rise, it holds services and sponsors activities all week long, from Bible readings and prayer groups through charities for the poor and dispossessed (such as earthquake victims) to campaigns against certain government policies.

Its doctrines are thoroughly Christian, with a strong focus on personal responsibility and social justice. Supported by donations from members, without help from abroad, it also operates a nursery school, a daycare center, an elementary school, and a seminary, reaching deeply into civil society.

Another, less noble, example is the Central Church in Shanghai, whose members, as Rob Schmitz notes, come from all walks of life to meet in a private apartment home, praying and chanting together in support of Christ, the Bible, love, community, and career. Highly modern in outlook and performance, the group uses flat-screen televisions, amplified sound, and rock music together with min-skirted hip-hop dancers to encourage "Jesus to come into my heart." Their leader, Preacher Jiang, used to be career criminal in one of the more notorious Shanghai triads and remains highly critical of the Party. He whips his congregation into a frenzy, praising God, Jesus, and the Bible, then suggests that all make monetary offerings in gratitude and to ensure additional grace, lest they be struck by disease and misfortune.

A case from a different section of the religious spectrum, also described by Rob Schmitz, is the unauthorized Buddhist temple in an unnamed, remote farming village several hours outside of Shanghai, run by a young meditation master, also unnamed, together with several apprentices. Consisting of five interconnected red-tile-roofed buildings that hold meeting rooms, living quarters, a canteen, and two worship halls, the temple grows gradually as donations come in. Spiritual seekers from the city, often in need of healing, visit there for a weekend pilgrimage, prostrate themselves multiple times, repent their sins, and sit together in meditation. The master, when he appears, exudes great authority and pronounces judgment on questions from the congregation, interpreting dreams, suggesting karmic cleansing for cases of disease, and giving advice on business matters. He then holds a special prayer ceremony, complete with chantings and prostrations, where everyone can pursue their particular issues, laying them at the foot of the Buddha in hope for resolution.

As far as Daoism is concerned, there are also underground groups, but they tend to remain rather well hidden. Typically associated with practices that even mainstream Daoists dismiss, such as sexual techniques and operative alchemy, they show up on occasion in internet blogs or are mentioned at conferences, but there is no clear reporting to date.

YouTube: "Underground Chinse Church Goes Public"

"Religion is on the Rise in China" (on churches after 5 minutes)

Read: Johnson, Ian. 2017. *The Souls of China: The Return of Religion after Mao*. New York: Pantheon Books.

Schmitz, Rob. 2016. *Street of Eternal Happiness: Big City Dreams along a Shanghai Road.* New York: Crown Publishers, chs. 4, 13.

Part 3

Culture

41. Censorship

Another level, where Daoism has an impact on China today goes beyond politics and economics and deals more with the general culture and outlook of the country. Here intellectuals and academics see issues of ethics, ecology, leadership, and more, evaluate them from a Daoist perspective, and make every effort to steer the country into a more sustainable, equitable, and creative direction. These efforts are hampered every step of the way, most importantly by the censorship that pervades all aspects of cultural and intellectual life.

The Party controls all media, both state-owned and private. All news agencies and broadcasting services belong to the state, including major newspapers, radio, and television stations. News are strictly controlled, and especially any form of protest anywhere in the world is usually blacked out. Thus, for example, when Hong Kong youths protested against mainland interference in their democratic process in 2015, occupying large parts of the city center, nobody in mainland China had a clue. Similarly, people are still surprised when, after going abroad, they first hear about the extent of suppression during the Tian'anmen democracy movement in 1989.

All content in publications and programming run by the private sector—books, CDs, videos, and magazines, featuring automobiles, gardening, computers, fashion, movies, and more—are subject to approval by censorship officials. At this point, this is usually a routine process, since writers and editors know the parameters of what is acceptable and self-censor with great efficiency.

The toughest and most complex censorship area is the internet. When it first became available in China in 1998, the government was delighted, seeing it as a major new way of influencing public opinion and establishing even more stringent controls. This proved not to be the case, and the state quickly took containing measures, establishing what they call the "golden shield," better known as the Great Firewall of China. This prevents some of the most common and most popular Western websites from operating in China, including Google, Gmail, Facebook, YouTube, Twitter, Instagram, and more—typically companies who, unlike Microsoft, refuse to allow the state to tamper with their content and limit freedom of expression.

This tampering is relatively easy, since there are few indigenous browsers and internet providers. Thus, keeping websites out and content limited is not as hard as it would be in a free country. On the other hand, people with a vested interest in access to Western information—notably businessmen and academics—get around the firewall by using virtual private networks (VPN), available for a few dollars a month and regularly advertised on the Chinese web. Tolerated by the government, yet under constant threat of closure, they create a virtual location for one's computing activity, in Australia, Europe, or America, that makes it look to the censors as if one were working overseas.

In addition, with the increase in cell phone usage—1.36 billion phones registered today—and the rise of new internet giants that include instant messaging like WeChat, communication has become instantaneous and pictures of natural disasters and social protests can go viral within minutes. As a result, the government today employs over two million people to monitor internet activity and watch for subversive content. This sometimes can be just a single word or common phrase. For example, during the Arab Spring in 2011, the word "jasmine"—part of Jasmine Revolution—was banned completely, making it impossible to shop for jasmine tea. Similarly, when the dissident Liu Xiaobo 刘晓波 was awarded the Nobel Peace Prize in 2010, the term "empty chair" was no longer acceptable.

On the proactive side, the state has also taken to bolster its online presence and popular image by hiring many thousands to regularly post positive comments about state policies on social media and wax enthusiastic for the new Party line of the China Dream.

YouTube: "China's Internet Censorship Explained"

Read: http://www.scmp.com/news/china/policies-politics/article/2110358/ chinas-religious-groups-brace-tighter-rules-curb

42. The *Daode jing*

Daoists are no strangers to state suppression and control. In fact, their earliest, central, and still most important classic was compiled to countermand just that. The *Daode jing*, linked with the sage Laozi, allegedly an archivist in the Zhou government during the 6th century BCE, is a short text of about 5000 characters. It is written in verse—not a rhyming, steady, rhythmic kind of verse, but a stylized prose that has strong parallels and regular patterns. Containing sayings, proverbs, and aphorisms, it typically presents sets of statements contrasted with tight punch lines. Often generic but never boring, the text radically and shamelessly proposes a way of life and style of rulership that is diametrically opposed to the reality at the time. For example,

> A huge thick tree grows from a tiny shoot.
> A nine-storied tower rises from a heap of earth.
> A thousand-mile journey starts with the first step.
> Act with intention and you will fail!
> Grasps hold firmly and you will lose!
> Therefore,
> The sage rests in non-action and never fails,
> Is without grasping and never loses. (ch. 64)

The Warring States (479-221 BCE) arose after centuries of declining Zhou rule, during which, due to iron-age technology and related economic changes, family-based feudal structures disintegrated. Each little duchy, hoping to rise to the status of kingdom and eventually gain hegemony, fought all others, progressively extending military service to create universal conscription and make every adult male into a soldier. The new military, moreover, reduced soldiers to the status of natural objects, children, or animals, and overall produced a brutally repressive system of sanctioned violence as the primary means of civil control.

A totalitarian and tyrannical regime that wielded comprehensive power, the system divided the population into groups of tens and fives, who not only had to spy on each other but would also be mutually liable, suffering the same punishment as the offender. "Anyone who failed to report a criminal activity would be chopped in two at the waist, while those who reported it received the same award as if they had taken the head of an enemy," the *Shiji* says.

War duly became an inescapable fact of life for everyone, the entire population conscripted into its service, farming in spring and summer and campaigning in fall and winter. Large infantry armies of up to 600,000 men fought each other to the death, creating destruction and devastation everywhere.

The *Daode jing* deplores this state of affairs and relentlessly rejects violence, proposing instead a withdrawing attitude, quiet living, and avoidance of official involvement. "Violent and fierce people," the text says, "do not die a natural death" (ch. 42), and adds, "Those who possess Dao turn away from weapons" (ch. 31). Focusing on the rhythmic and harmonious patterns of nature as opposed to social and military efforts, the text proposes the derivation of identity, both personal and communal, from the larger environment and the greater universe rather than from social conventions and political power structures.

It accordingly emphasizes the activation of proper cosmic energy flow together with a deep-seated respect for, and honoring of, the earth with its mountains and rivers as markers of space as well as of the heavens with sun and moon as the setters of time. Beyond that, the *Daode jing* supports several key personal values, such as an ease and flow of life in nonaction, social flexibility expressed as softness and weakness, individual authenticity or living in genuine truth, as well as humility, simplicity, and sufficiency—knowing who we are in relation to nature and society, what we can and cannot do in any given situation, and when and what it means that there is enough.

YouTube: "Minute Faith—Taoism"

Read: Kohn, Livia. 2017. *Pristine Affluence: Daoist Roots in the Stone Age*. St. Petersburg, Fla.: Three Pines Press.

Kohn, Livia, and Michael LaFargue, eds. 1998. *Lao-tzu and the Tao-te-ching*. Albany: State University of New York Press.

43. Philosophical Adaptations

The key concepts and values of the *Daode jing* have played an important role throughout Chinese history and, especially in the 20th century, served as a major way of coming to terms with Western thought.

For example, the renowned thinker Hu Shi 胡適 (1891-1962; see above) linked Daoist ideas of cosmic unfolding to Darwinian evolution, while political philosophers Guo Moruo 郭沫若 (1892-1978) and Hou Wailu 侯外廬 (1903-1987) argued that its fundamental outlook, particularly as expressed in its notion of *qi* and the flow of yin and yang, was essentially materialist and could thus be understood as a Chinese precursor of Marxism. They saw passages like, "Attain complete emptiness, maintain steadfast stillness" (ch. 16), usually thought to refer to practices of self-cultivation, as reflections of an early materialist outlook that focused on the here and now as opposed to some far-off deity.

In contrast, idealist thinkers Li Taifeng 李泰奉 (1987-1972) and Guan Feng 關峰 (1919-2005) did not see sufficient evidence for materialism but understood the *Daode jing* to reflect an ancient form of objective idealism that divides the world dualistically into visible reality and a formless, underlying ground. In his *Laozi tong* 老子通 (Penetrating the *Laozi*) of 1984, Guan Feng argues against seeing Dao as the underlying material mechanism of the cosmos and reads it more along the lines of ancient Greek *nous*.

Similarly, Feng Youlan 馮友蘭 (1895-1990) understands it as the origin of the myriad phenomena, the core of all transformations, an imperceptible transcendent quality that is neither this nor that, but the powerful source of both, presence or being (*you* 有) and absence or nonbeing (*wu* 無). Chen Guying 陳鼓應 (b. 1935) concurs and, in his commentaries and discussions of the *Daode jing*, not only relates it to Western thinkers such as Nietzsche but also insists on its deep ontology, describing Dao as a metaphysical reality that cannot be named yet serves as a regulating principle and standard for human behavior.

In a yet different vein, the Daoist philosopher Ren Jiyu 任繼愈 (1916-2009) reads the text in connection to the Marxist thinker Friedrich Engels (1820-1895) and his view that close observation serves as the material base of all theories. In contrast Ren proposes that *Daode jing* passages, such as "Know the world without going out of doors" (ch. 47), indicate a preference for theory and speculation over direct, scientific observation. He then evaluates this as a deficiency, noting that it was a mistake to break away from the investigation of material things and forms of energy in favor of trying to understand the world as such.

The literary scholar and novelist Qian Zhongshu 錢鍾書 (1910-1998), educated also in Oxford and Paris and a popular lecturer in the West, in his 1980s collection of vignettes and personal musings called *Guanzhui bian* 管錐編 (Tube and Awl Chapters), has nineteen entries on the *Daode jing*. Unlike other thinkers, he begins with the very first line of the work, "The Dao that can be told is not the constant Dao," and focuses on issues of language and semiotics, thereby opening the text to a deep metaphysical probing without neglecting textual details.

Adducing numerous Western thinkers from Plato through Spinoza and Hobbes to Hegel and Nietzsche as well as major literary figures such as Dante and Goethe, he argues like Ferdinand de Saussure (1857-1913) that language is different from speech and consists of the signifier (word, symbol, sign) and the signified (thought, idea, object) in an arbitrary yet logically structured relationship. Naming and signification form an essential aspect of world-building, a world that in essence rests on a supreme underlying truth: the ineffable, formless Dao, leading to a situation where "who knows does not speak; who speaks does not know" (ch. 56). Ultimately insufficient to express this truth yet necessary for its transmission, language with all its intricacies and inadequacies is a core issue not only for writers but also for thinkers and humanity at large.

YouTube: "An Interview with Timothy Creek"

"Who Was Qian Zhongshu?"

Read: Creek, Timothy. 2015. *The Intellectual in Modern China*. Cambridge: Cambridge University Press.

44. Academia

Since the founding of the People's Republic, Daoist as much as other intellectual activity first shrank then ceased, to renew only after Deng Xiaoping's drive toward modernization. Even then, libraries were closed or heavily censored, intellectual activities were limited to universities and tightly supervised, and the main focus was on Marxism-Leninism. The field of Daoist Studies was close to nonexistent, religion being still considered an "opiate of the people," and any discussions of classical Daoist concepts and values was counterrevolutionary.

Gradually this changed, slowly during the 1990s, vigorously in the 2000s. Now scholars engage in Daoist Studies at numerous universities, affiliated institutes, and research organizations, as well as at Academies of Social Sciences. They hold meetings and conferences, engage in cooperative projects, work together and exchange ideas, generally following state directives as issued by the Bureau of Religious Affairs, which in turn bows to the Department of Propaganda and the Cultural Planning Committee. While some scholars are Daoist believers, most pursue religious studies for the sake of academic knowledge, while yet others belong to political organizations propagating atheism.

The oldest academic institution with a core focus on Daoism is the Religion Department of Sichuan University, established in 1980 under the leadership of Qing Xitai 卿希泰 (b. 1928), author of numerous works on Daoist history and thought. The Department encourages Daoist Studies in all dimensions. A formal master's degree in Religion was established in 1983, and a doctorate in

1991. Also since 1982, it has published a journal, *Zongjiao xue yanjiu* 宗教學研究 (Religious Studies).

In 2009, Qing Xitai further established a specialized Laozi Institute 老子研究院, greatly enhancing the study of the *Daode jing* in history and today, among intellectuals as well as practitioners, within Han Chinese culture and in relation to minorities. Supported by the Ministry of Education and various provincial institutions, the Institute has received international funding for over thirty major research projects and published large numbers of books and articles, some of which received awards for outstanding research.

Similarly, Peking University has a long tradition of religious studies. Today it teaches aspects of Daoism in the Philosophy, History, and Chinese Departments as well as in the Center for Religious Studies, established in 1989, and since 1995 the Department of Religion. Its goal is the study of religion in a scientific and objective manner, employing a critical approach to both its historical development and organizational and doctrinal structures, and paying special attention to its interaction with various aspects of culture. It also sponsors a Center for Daoist Studies 道家研究中心, established in 2012 under the leadership of Chen Guying (b. 1935), now headed by Wang Bo 王博 (b. 1969). It is home to many excellent scholars and an increasing number of Ph. D. students.

Besides these two prominent centers and many other departments at universities, an important venue of study is the Chinese Academy of Social Sciences (CASS). Established in 1977 by separating research units on philosophy and society from the overarching Academy of Sciences, it is China's most comprehensive research organization and closely affiliated with the central government. It consists of over 90 research centers in charge of 105 national academic communities, staffed by over 3200 resident scholars. Several among its thirty-five research institutes, including those on philosophy, history, and world religions, also employ Daoist specialists. Working within state-approved guidelines and increasingly subject to political interference, many of them are in contact with Western scholars and, as much as the state allows, join international conferences on Daoist Studies for productive exchange and mutual support.

In addition, many scholars also join nationwide research societies, such as the Laozi Daoist Culture Research Society 老子道学文化研究会. Bringing together academics, clergy, and lay enthusiasts, it is present throughout the country, connecting to civil and religious groups. Encouraging a wide range of approaches and opinions, its central goal goes beyond academic and theoretical understanding: the creation of a new Daoism that brings ancient concepts into the modern world, enhances traditional ethics, and contributes to harmonious social development. Using the correct Party-speak and limiting itself to general discussions, it sponsors seminars, conferences, and workshops, representing a tame but influential aspect of the continued expansion of Daoist ideas.

YouTube: "University in China"

Read: Ding, Huang. 2000. "The Study of Daoism in China Today." In *Daoism Handbook*, edited by Livia Kohn, 765-91. Leiden: Brill.

45. Liu Xiaogan

An excellent example of a successful Chinese academic with a vested interest in promoting Daoist ideals is Liu Xiaogan 刘笑敢. Born in Henan in 1947, he graduated from high school in Tianjin but, before he could enroll at university in 1968, he was sent down to the countryside to "learn from the peasants." Ending up in Inner Mongolia and suffering through famine and other hardships, he made his way to its capital of Hohhot and enrolled in the Chinese Department of its Normal University in 1973. Graduating with a Master's degree, he joined the Philosophy Department of Peking University in 1978, earning his Ph. D. in 1985.

The next few years he spent as a post-doctoral fellow in the U. S., receiving grants from Michigan, Harvard, and Princeton Universities. In 1993, he became professor of philosophy at the National University of Singapore, from where he transferred to the Chinese University of Hong Kong in 2001. Gradually drawn back into the mainland academic scene, he soon came to serve as adviser for various institutions and Daoist research centers, often working as adjunct professor since his retirement in 2012.

His main work focuses on Daoist thought. While he has done his share of politically correct and widely acceptable textual studies, identifying different styles and layers in ancient documents, he has also—sagely beyond the Party's reach—been vocal about government interference and micromanagement. His main argument rests on bringing two key *Daode jing* values to the fore and applying them in modern life: naturalness (*ziran* 自然) and nonaction (*wu-wei* 无为).

Naturalness, also called self-being or spontaneity, means resting within one's inherent natural self, which works perfectly within the self-generating and self-organizing order of the universe. Dao itself is essential naturalness; its power, as the *Daode jing* says, "is not due to some outside command, but rests in constant self-being" (ch. 51). Within society, it applies to all: people do best what comes naturally, what they are trained for, and what they have control over. To facilitate that, moreover, the job of the ruler is to rest in nonaction, like Dao itself being there to nourish, sustain, and assist while letting the people follow their own accord. Government should be open to all beings and the natural world and deal with them flexibly and fluidly, facilitating without imposing.

Liu Xiaogan applies this in concrete terms to modern society. As an example, he presents the case of a farmer who is about to modernize his farm. If he looks around and finds many modern methods being applied, understands the rationale behind them and their advantages for everyone concerned, and if he has both the time to investigate the new methods and the money to make the investment, then the time is right, the new development matches the criteria of naturalness, and things in all likelihood will proceed smoothly. If, on the other hand, he works only for egotistic profit to the detriment of everyone else, or if a government or corporation forces him to change his basic methods at a moment when he has neither time nor money, then he is going against the natural flow and likely headed for trouble. "The principle of naturalness," Liu says, "always prefers inner dynamism to external force."

It means that things grow and develop in their own way and to the benefit of all, that humans work best in alignment with the natural patterns to fulfill themselves and avoid harming others. The job of the state, then, is to rest in nonaction: take a big step back and occupy a position of *laissez-faire*, let people work in the way they know best. By extension, and this is where the Party line is crossed, the state should encourage them to engage in self-determination and, by extension, self-government.

YouTube: "Eastern Philosophy: Wu Wei"

Read: Liu, Xiaogan. 1998. "Naturalness (*Tzu-jan*), the Core Value in Taoism: Its Ancient Meaning and Its Significance Today." In *Lao-tzu and the Tao-te-ching*, edited by Livia Kohn and Michael LaFargue, 211-28. Albany: State University of New York Press.

Liu, Xiaogan. 2001. "Nonaction and the Environment Today: A Conceptual and Applied Study of Laozi's Philosophy." In *Daoism and Ecology: Ways within a Cosmic Landscape*, edited by Norman Girardot, James Miller, and Liu Xiaogan, 315-40. Cambridge, Mass.: Harvard University Press, Center for the Study of World Religions.

46. Leadership

The ideal Daoist leader is a sagely agents who embodies Dao and serves his community unselfishly. As the *Daode jing* has it, "The best person is like water; water is good: it benefits all beings and does not compete" (ch. 8). Like water, which is invisible and only takes form through its container, Daoist leaders embody several major virtues—all strangers to Party and state officials today—altruism, humility, flexibility, transparency, honesty, and gentle persistence as well as non-competition, kindness, faithfulness, and competence.

They are particularly good at the three treasures of the *Daode jing*: caring or fundamental kindness, thriftiness or frugality, and "not daring to be ahead of the world" (ch. 67). As the text says, they always "place themselves in the background, put themselves away, and have no personal interests" (ch. 7).

Good leaders never engage in self-justification or strut in the limelight, remaining consistently without pride, possessiveness, and personal acclaim (ch. 22). Possessing the relevant knowledge, skills, and expertise for their tasks, they may have a clear mission yet remain free from personal desires and never take interfering action. Without exerting force or control, they inspire people to do their best, closely matching nature and the continuously changing circumstances of life. As much as life is a fluid configuration or a field of flux, leadership is a set of experientially located and responsive relational skills-in-process. As a result, leaders work with efficacy rather than for effect, blending energies as they serve as facilitators, communicators, and team builders.

In contrast to Warring States tyrants and Communist officials, ideal Daoist leaders exert only a minimal influence on their subjects, employing soft tactics, such as persuasion, empowerment, modeling, collaboration, and service, never resorting to force or violence. They encourage citizens to take ownership of and responsibility for their tasks. Demonstrating creativity and flexibility in a life dedicated to service, they promote harmony with nature and others.

In sum, Daoist leaders are democratic as opposed to autocratic, *laissez-faire* as opposed to coercive, service-oriented as opposed to domineering, and charismatic as opposed to bureaucratic, the highest type as defined in the *Daode jing*:

> The highest—you don't even know they're there.
> The next—you love and praise them.
> The next—you fear them.
> The lowest—you despise them. (ch. 17)

The highest leadership, therefore, is consensual and fluid; it focuses on the well-being of the entire group. Leaders—competent, intelligent, strong, and healthy—receive deference and make decisions yet remain in the background, so that "the people say they did it all themselves," as the *Daode jing* has it (ch. 17).

All other leaders focus on deficiency, always striving for more, higher, better. While some do so with gentle methods and get positive results, so that the people "love and praise them," most have power rather than authority, that is, they exercise forceful mastery over others whose compliance is often unwilling, engendering fear and loathing. They derive it socially from organizational membership and community networks, economically from control over production and exchange of subsistence, and militarily from coercing compliance with superior strength through police and secret services.

The despised tyrants, finally have complete control, defined as the ability to restrain or block access to resources, mediated by a hierarchy of loyal followers and a tightly structured bureaucracy. Ruling with brute force, they derive political power from various forms of sanctioned violence, be it the forced eviction of people from their houses, the radical limitation of access to information, the bending and twisting of civil justice, or the incarceration of dissidents.

YouTube: "The Tao of Leadership"

Read: Heider, John. 1985. *Tao of Leadership*. Atlanta: Humanics New Age.

Lee, Yueh-Ting, Ai-Guo Han, Tammy K. Byron, and Hong-Xia Fan. 2008. "Daoist Leadership: Theory and Application." In *Leadership and Management in China*, edited by Chao-Chuan Chen and Yueh-Ting Lee, 83-107. Cambridge: Cambridge University Press.

47. Dissent

Tyrannies, by their very nature, engender dissent. Both in traditional China and today, this comes in various distinct forms, ranging from the covert to the open, the subtle to the radical, and also including what may be called accidental criticism. In this case, the person steps into a position of dissent without actually meaning to do so.

An example, documented by Liao Yiwu, is the composer Wang Xilin 王西麟, in the 1990s a rising star on the Chinese music scene. He had written various symphonies that were widely praised and also performed internationally. In 2000, he was under contract with the Beijing Municipal Government to conduct his music in a series of concerts. At the first rehearsal in November, he greeted the orchestra and, among more generic welcoming remarks, acknowledged the end of the 20th century and declared that Communism was over and done with.

This faux-pas cost him a few years of his career. The Party declared him a counterrevolutionary, banned his musical works, made him write confession after self-condemning confession, had him accuse himself in self-criticism sessions before the orchestra, and placed him under house arrest. He recanted and laid low, and after a few years was allowed to perform again

On the other end of the spectrum, the most radical form of dissent is intentional, open resistance that may even result in, armed rebellion. Daoists and other religious groups were responsible for quite a few uprisings throughout Chinese history, usually when times were rough: leadership failing, corruption rampant, and resources scarce. The first well documented case involving Daoists is the Dao of Great Peace (Taiping dao 太平道), who rose up in 184 CE, causing the end of Han-dynasty rule. Many others have followed, often toppling governments, which explains why the Party today is so exceedingly nervous about mass assemblies and religious organizations.

A second, slightly less radical expression of dissent is removal: leaving the area of tyrannical, totalitarian rule and setting up an alternative community elsewhere. The prime example in ancient Daoism is the growth of primitivist or anarchist groups as described in the *Zhuangzi*. They moved to the remote countryside and established stone-age style communities that eschewed all technology, culture, and governance. Today, removal means getting out of China altogether, and often dissidents, like the well-known artist Ai Weiwei 艾未未, or controversial religious figures. e. g., the Falungong leader Li Hongzhi, end up living in the U. S.

A much calmer way of dealing with dissent is inner emigration—a (not entirely positive) term coined with regard to German writers who chose to remain in country and keep quiet under the Nazis. In Daoism, we find this reaction preferred by Zhuangzi, who compared rulers to wild tigers and refused to serve in office, instead "dragging his tail in the mud" on his country estate. Other Daoist intellectuals who took this route are the Seven Sages of the Bamboo Grove. Living in unstable times in the early 3rd century CE, they refrained from official involvement, getting drunk and writing poetry in the country instead.

Today, the pattern holds true for many religious and spiritual seekers as well as for underground churches and some civil rights lawyers. Rather than risking life and limb and endangering their families, they are well aware of what is going on but keep their criticism below danger threshold. They represent, as the Party knows all too well, a potential powder keg should things start to go wrong. They are observed, but largely left alone.

A yet different alternative is the publication of dissenting statements under cover of something else. In ancient China, this was typically achieved in literature and philosophy, most importantly among Confucian literati who rejected the authoritarian rule of certain dynasties but did not dare to voice their opinions openly. Interpreting honored classics or writing beautiful poems, they would use certain phrases and metaphors in a highly circumspect way that carried one meaning to government agents and another to other their fellow literati.

Today, a similar phenomenon, as Emily Parker describes, appears among bloggers. Increasingly banned from the mainstream internet, they either try to get their information abroad where it can be posted, use short-lived but potent microblogs that escape detection, or—like their literati forebears—write one thing and mean another, thus avoiding the censor. An example is a popular blog about Qingming 清明, the festival of the dead, that usually falls in late May. Expressing sadness and deploring the loss of loved ones, hoping for their well-being in the afterlife and a successful rebirth, the blog in fact talks about the June 4 Tian'anmen massacre and encourages people to continue the democratic mission. While creating a dissenting underground, this way yet falls short of open impact.

Open criticism, then, is the realm of vocal dissenters, usually artists, writers, academics, or lawyers, many of whom studied abroad where they learned just how much China lacks basic freedom. They are often spurred into action when ordinary people become victims of the system—such as the killing of students at Tian'anmen, the faulty response after the Sichuan earthquake, the forced eviction of people from their homes, the suppression of Muslims in Xinjiang, and more.

One example, as described by Liao Yiwu, is Ding Zilin 丁子霖, a Beijing philosophy professor whose son was killed in 1989. In response, she founded the Tian'anmen Mothers, challenging the government's whitewashing of the event and demanding rehabilitation. She, as much as other dissidents, continue their work despite constant police harassment, house arrests, detention, and forced vacations from major political centers during sensitive times

The most prominent Chinese dissident today is the poet and Nobel Peace Prize winner Liu Xiaobo, whose work, too, began with Tian'anmen but from there expanded into unceasing defense of the disenfranchised. His death in July 2017 was noticed mainly abroad—in China only very few people even know his name.

Similarly unremarked in the country was the mass incarceration and systematic persecution of civil rights lawyers on July 9, 2015, known as the 709 group. A central hub of dissent that holds the critical network together, they were pushed to sign papers that made them tow the Party line and refrain from public dissent. Some, fearing for their families, complied, and are now treading more softly, while others got stuck in prison, suffering physical torture and mental abuse.

YouTube: "Liu Xiaobo, Nobel Peace Prize Winner"

"Chinese Bloggers Ask the U.S. to Heal Tear Down the Great Firewal"

Read: Parker, Emily. 2014. *Now I Know Who My Comrades Are: Voices from the Internet Underground*. New York: Sarah Crichton Books.

Liao, Yiwu. 2009. *The Corpse Walker: Real-Life Stories, China from the Bottom Up*. New York: Anchor, 93-111. 214-29.

https://www.nytimes.com/2017/07/25/magazine/the-lonely-crusade-of-chinas-human-rights-lawyers.html?mcubz=0

48. Education

A key factor in the state control of culture and people's thinking is education. In China, almost all schools are state-run, under the supervision of the Ministry of Education. Rigid in discipline, organization, and structure, they are a means of political indoctrination for the purpose of ruling the people rather than for the development of the individual person. Instilling patriotic slogans and propagating the Party's take on history and politics, they intentionally prevent any form of critical thinking. Chinese schools may produce high scores in math and science, but they do so due to intense study, regimentation, competition, and standardized testing. They coerce even little children with a mixture of punishments, threats, and bribes, making them sit upright and still while chanting self-hypnotic verses like "I am a good child, little hands always in place, little feet refined, little ears listening well," thereby creating "little soldiers" (Chu 2017).

Everyone has to attend school for at least nine years in their home town as defined by their household registration: there is no home schooling and no leaving the school district. The overall system matches the American division into six (in some places five) years of primary education, followed by three (or four) years of middle or junior high school.

While 80 percent of children make it that far, about 50 percent (mostly in the cities), after grueling entrance examinations—on occasion assisted by parental bribes—go on to high school. 37 percent attend university.

Elementary and middle schools are the bailiwick of local, i. e., county and municipal, administrations. High schools and most universities are run by provincial governments, and 110 institutions of higher learning—including the most prestigious ones—answer directly to the Ministry of Education. There is a growing market for private colleges, mostly practice-oriented or vocational, but they still have to submit to government accreditation and control.

Among university students, the best and brightest get to study abroad, to the tune of half a million every year, most of whom (300,000) are in the U. S., specializing in science, technology, and business. The return rate is up to 37 percent from a meager 15 a few years ago, but this still means that two thirds of the brightest and best educated do not contribute to innovation in country.

Innovation happens when education is open and flexible. For example, David Zalik, a notable innovator featured in *Forbes* magazine, skipped high school and went directly to college, where he assembled PCs on his own to buy a car so he could impress his dates. Eventually he built a computer company he sold for a few million dollars at age 22, moving on to greater and more innovative schemes from there.

This could never happen in China (or in Europe, for that matter). Leaders and educators alike are now realizing just how "trite, empty, and deadlocked" the system is, and to what degree rote learning and strict regimentation of thinking and behavior kill initiative and stymy inventiveness. They have begun some reforms, documented in what Lenora Chu calls the White Bible, an official guideline for schools that encourages more openness and creativity. However, all this remains ineffective as long as household registration and entrance examinations are still in place.

Daoists in this context propose—very much along the lines described by Johannes Gasser, founder of the Flow Academy in Switzerland—to follow the natural inclinations and internal rhythms of the child, enticing and seducing toward knowledge while engaging body, heart, and mind. More specifically, they recommend applying the methods and ideals described in the *Daode jing* to let children unfold their inherent, congenital wisdom and cultivate inspirational and creative thinking. Just as "good governance is like water," so good guidance for youngsters should be smooth and easy, using teaching materials and methods that remain simple and straightforward, allowing the children to grow at their own rate and fulfilling their own unique potentials.

This closely echoes the thinking of Maria Montessori, who like Laozi was a careful observer of nature, people, and events, and similarly saw the universe as an interconnected harmony of symbiotic elements. Both believe that the challenges of life, society, education, and leadership must be solved by adherence to the natural laws of cosmic order and equally enjoy the use of water's flow as a metaphor.

A cosmic connection to the "etheric world" is also central in the educational thought of Rudolf Steiner, the founder of the Waldorf schools, where children learn through play and do at least as much with their hands and bodies as with their brains. The first Waldorf school in China was founded in 2004 by a couple of elementary school teachers in Chengdu.

They first heard about the system in 1994 from Australian tourists, who came to eat at the restaurant they were running at the time. They underwent formal training in England, got state approval, and went into business. After struggling for several years, the school has become quite successful and today has 300 students, from kindergarten through 8th grade, plus a 5-year waiting list. Country-wide, there are over 200 kindergartens and about 30 elementary schools that follow the Waldorf model.

The schools attend closely to each child's individual needs, promote creative exploration, and foster respect, caring, and community. Learning comes after being human; training supports the unfolding of natural gifts, skills, and tendencies. Unlike mainstream education, they raise people with a strong moral compass and cheerful self-confidence.

YouTube: "Summer Camps China" (Waldorf)

"Chinese School Episode 1" (BBC)

Read: Chu, Lenora. 2017. *Little Soldiers: An American Boy, a Chinese School, and the Global Race to Achieve.* New York: Harper.

Gasser, Johannes. 2011. "Re-sourcive Pedagogy: Teaching and Education as Vital Energy Flow." In *Living Authentically: Daoist Contributions to Modern Psychology*, edited by Livia Kohn, 234-54. Dunedin, Fla.: Three Pines Press.

Kohn, Livia, 2018. *The Dao of Parenting: Daoist Wisdom Meets Modern Psychology*. St. Petersburg, Fla.: Three Pines Press

Zhao, Yong. 2014. *Who's Afraid of the Big Bad Dragon: Why China Has the Best (and Worst) Education System in the World.* San Francisco: Jossey -Bass.

https://www.newyorker.com/magazine/2014/02/03/class-consciousness

49. Ethics

The moral compass in China is in serious decline. A hot topic these days, this state is the result of a long development, beginning with the Opium Wars and (Christian-inspired) Taiping Rebellion in the mid-19th century. With hardly a break from civil wars, rebellions, foreign invasions, and Communist campaigns, the country suffered incessantly from violent conflict. This not only has decimated its population, especially the educated elite, but more importantly is sending a strong message to the people that human life is cheap and that no cost is too high for survival.

The state-enforced sterilization of women and abortion of unborn children during the one-child policy and the still continuing killing of citizens—be they dissenters, Falungong practitioners, or just unwilling to surrender their homes to greedy officials—does nothing to change the overarching cultural pattern. Add to this the doctrine of radical materialism, the rigid and unforgiving educational system, the strong sense of entitlement of only children—both pampered and burdened by family expectations—as well as the rampant competition in a feverish economy, and you have the spiritual vacuum we see today, complete with an utter lack of moral responsibility.

This is particularly evident from several recent cases. A young man helps an old woman after she falls when leaving a bus, escorting her to the hospital and even paying her minor bill. She promptly sues him, and the judge sentences him to pay a fine, arguing that only someone with a guilty conscience would pay another person's bill. This shows that even leaders in the society cannot even imagine an altruistic or selfless act!

Another case is the toddler run over by a van, documented on YouTube. Not only does the van not stop, but for a good half hour people pass by right and left, ignoring the injured child. One woman, taking out the trash, finally pays attention and gets her treated, but the moral decrepitude is evident from the numbers of people who just turn the other way.

Not just strangers, but also family members have no regard for each other any longer, requiring official edicts to perform basic kindness. Thus, in 2013, the government passed a formal law that children must visit their elderly parents often "enough," leading to a slew of lawsuits among close relatives. The contrast to traditional family values could not be starker.

The Party has recognized the issue and is striving to re-establish classical moral values among the population. It relies dominantly on the Confucian system, which acknowledges five personal and five social virtues. The five personal virtues include honesty and trust as a central value, followed by propriety—a sense of decency and respect—and wisdom or sympathetic understanding, The last two are the best-known Confucian virtues benevolence and righteousness, that is, interpersonal goodwill and taking social responsibility.

The five social virtues center on the core value of reciprocity, which means that each partner in any interaction matches the other's attitude and deeds. From here, there are two pairs, focusing on family and state, respectively. Within the family, children are supposed to practice filial piety, not only obeying their parents but putting their well-being first. The parents, on the other hand, should be kind and caring, supporting their child's growth and development. Within the state, subjects owe loyalty to the ruler, who in his turn should demonstrate superior virtue or moral excellence. If one partner in this set-up fails to fulfill his part, the other has the right, and even the duty, to complain, criticize, admonish, and even rise in rebellion.

Historically, Daoists adopted this overall system but expanded it beyond the social framework and into more cosmic dimensions, at the same time anchoring the virtues deep in the individual's body and linking them to prevalent negative emotions as well as to the five Buddhist precepts, which they adopted in the middle ages.

Thus, trust or honesty resides in the spleen and stomach, right in the center of the abdomen—what we might call gut feelings. It overcomes the tendency to worry and connects to the precept against lying, creating fictional presentations of self and reality. Propriety, next, belongs to the heart and links to the precept against intoxication, limiting the impact of excessive exuberance while supporting mental and social clarity.

Wisdom emerges from the kidneys and is part of the prohibition against stealing, reducing fear of survival while encouraging the core Daoist realization of sufficiency or "knowing when it is enough." In addition, benevolence flows from the liver and indicates the overcoming of anger and aggression, manifest in the precept against killing. Righteousness, finally, rests with lungs, reduces sadness and encourages chastity, linked with the precept against sexual misconduct or licentiousness.

As regards the social virtues, Daoists see reciprocity, caring, support, and moral awareness in a much wider context, including not only humans but also other beings as well as the natural world. They encourage extending gratitude, respect, and kindness not only to the people of immediate concern, but also to humanity at large. Going beyond that, they also include the various animals and plants that provide sustenance and nurturing, as well as the trees, mountains, rivers, oceans, and other natural entities—all the way to the stars—that make life on the planet possible.

YouTube: "Chinese Ethics and Moral Dilemmas"

"Redefining China's Family: Elderly"

"Chinese Child Got Hit by Car Twice"

Read: Ivanhoe, P. J. 2000. *Confucian Moral Self Cultivation*. Indianapolis: Hackett Publishing.

Kohn, Livia. 2004. *Cosmos and Community: The Ethical Dimension of Daoism*. Cambridge, Mass.: Three Pines Press.

Leightner, Jonathan Edward. 2017. *Ethics, Efficiency, and Macroeconomics in China: From Mao to Xi*. New York: Routledge.

50. Ecology

Given this ethical stance, it is not surprising that Daoism also offers a practical philosophy of ecological living. Central here are its key values of nonaction and naturalness (*ziran*), especially since the latter is also the modern word for "nature." Multicentric and supportive of all, Daoism provides an ethos that supports the expression of each beings' integrity, deferring to all relevant environmental conditions while establishing efficacious and fruitful integration.

Modern Chinese ecologists adopt Daoist thought to see nature and naturalness in close connection as the unceasing movement of things, manifest in the continued ordering and disintegration or ongoing entropy of life, the organic chemical transformations in living matter, and the homeostatic processes of the healthy body. Most pertinently, they see in Daoism an archaic wisdom that understands life as universally interconnected or interbeing, values diversity as a fundamental condition for flourishing, and insists on the essential compatibility of all life forms as well as the need for humans to treat other species with respect. For them, Daoism represents the appreciation of nature not as a teleological realization of a fixed trajectory but as a continuous waymaking that supports life in all its forms.

To heal the world and treat the many environmental problems that ail China today, ecologists take recourse to classic Daoist values such as tolerance, integrity, and respect. They also encourage the application of non-processes (*wu* 无) to eliminate the urge toward exploitation and control. These include non-desire, the embracing of sufficiency; non-knowledge, a relaxed, unprincipled, and even anarchic knowing; and, most importantly, nonaction interpreted as non-interference.

This does not mean inaction or letting things go wild, but perpetual creativity where nothing is not done forcefully, the development and maintenance of steadfast congruence. Each being should follow its own accord and connect to others and the natural world without imposing on them, living in a non-confrontational way, making changes gently, slowly, and consciously in alignment with all and without dramatic effects.

In concrete terms, this means respecting natural features and using resources sparingly, applying renewable energy whenever possible. Examples include building houses that blend into the natural setting, designing gardens that enhance and highlight natural forms, training animals with gentleness rather than with force to enhance their natural powers. Another example, described by Janine Benyus, is the mode of "do nothing" farming, pioneered in Japan by Fukuoka Masanobu, author of *One Straw Revolution*.

Instead of planting just one annual crop, aiding it with fertilizers and pesticides, he sows clover seeds into his field of standing rice, followed a little while later by seeds of rye and barley. When the rice is ready for harvest, he cuts and threshes it, then throws the straw back over the field. The clover, already well established, smothers weeds and keeps nitrogen active. Soon rye and barley shoot up. Once they are harvested, he again starts the cycle by sowing rice. He developed the method, which is increasingly also practiced in China, with the age-old Daoist method of "diminish and again diminish" (*Daode jing* 48), arriving at the perfect nonaction way of farming: using no machines, no prepared fertilizer, and no chemicals, it yet yields the same or more than standard methods.

In terms of innovation, the close Daoist relationship to and observation of nature encourages the growing field of biomimicry or biomimetics, using natural patterns and systems as models for technological innovation. Thus, for example, synthetic fabrics imitate the biological structure of natural weaves, dyes use structural coloration instead of pigmentation, building designs copy termite mounds to control temperature and moisture, and mussels become the model for ways to create underwater adherence.

Another key feature is recycling, in China still in its infancy although it used to form a major part of traditional living. Worldwide, on the other hand, China is an essential contributor, notably in the areas of heavy metals and paper. Thus, as Adam Minter documents, a good half of all the copper wires and metal rods in those innumerable new Chinese high rises are recycled from American discards while the cardboard boxes, in which your Amazon order arrives, come from American paper recycled in China. The industry began when China's exports grew exponentially, shippers wondering what in the world they could put into all those empty containers going back across the ocean: scrap was the obvious answer, and a successful, multi-billion-dollar industry was born.

Today, with massive levels of pollution, an overall rise in the standard of living, and increasing wages for Chinese workers, this is coming to an end. After importing 26 million tons of waste products in 2016, in 2017, the government announced that China would no longer be "the world's garbage dump," refusing to take on twenty-four different kinds of solid waste, most importantly metals, plastic bottles, and paper products.

Since the ban went into effect on January 1, 2018, Western countries have been scrambling to process garbage piling up in large heaps and enact new legislation to reduce waste. Some are now sending their materials to other developing nations or begin to recycle at home, but the infrastructure is not there, and the volume nowhere near matches Chinese capacities. Overall, the new Chinese policy is bound to give a major boost to environmental awareness worldwide, providing one—in this case, positive—example on how China is changing the world.

YouTube: "Daoism and Ecology"

"Junkyard Planet"

Read: Birdwhistell, Joanne D. 2001. "Ecological Questions for Daoist Thought: Contemporary Issues and Ancient Texts." In *Daoism and Ecology: Ways within a Cosmic Landscape*, edited by Norman Girardot, James Miller, and Liu Xiaogan, 23-44. Cambridge, Mass.: Harvard University Press, Center for the Study of World Religions.

Benyus, Janine M. 1998. *Biomimicry: Innovation Inspired by Nature*. New York: HarperCollins.

Miller, James. 2017. *China's Green Religion: Daoism and the Quest for a Sustainable Future*. New York: Columbia University Press.

Minter, Adam. 2013. *Junkyard Planet: Travels in the Billion-Dollar Trash Trade*. New York: Bloomsbury.

51. Sustainable Business

Another impact of greater environmental awareness a new level of business thinking today that focuses on solving urgent planetary issues while yet providing employment to thousands of people and making a profit. Traditionally, entrepreneurial wisdom placed profit and shareholder gains at the center of all business decisions. In contrast, now more and more executives recognize that we live in a world torn by utterly unnecessary, wasteful, and degrading rifts—economic, political, ethnic, religious, and more. As a result, they place ecological and social issues at the forefront, doing business in such a way that benefits accrue in all three areas—company, society, ecology—or what people now call the triple bottom line.

A catchphrase in this context is corporate social responsibility, signifying a higher level of societal expectations toward corporations, their operating modes, products, and impact. It is no longer sufficient for companies to minimize harm in the conduct of their business; rather, they have to take an active role in the support of social and environmental progress, and even come to envision new ways of doing and living.

This closely matches Daoist ideas. As already the *Daode jing* has,

To produce things and to rear them;
To produce but not to take possession of them;
To act, but not to rely on one's own ability;
To lead them, but not to master them—
This is called profound and secret virtue. (ch. 10)
Do not elevate the worthy, and people will not compete.
Do not value rare goods, and people will not steal.
Do not display the desirable, and people will not be confused. (ch. 3)

This also plays out in workplace values. As Mitroff and Denton document (2012), American businesses run by ethnic Chinese of a traditional Confucian background make the Golden Rule their number one priority. They believe that a few core ethical values, more concrete and applicable than spiritual notions such as faith, are sufficient to produce and run ethical companies. Creating values-based organizations, they keep their vocabulary neutral, focus on actions rather than words, and treat all people with deep respect, as whole persons. Extending traditional Chinese family ethics into the workplace, they see their employees and shareholders as members of an extended family, placing profit second after personal interaction.

This, moreover, enhances the bottom line and increases profits. Employees who feel valued and have a strong moral compass, working in ethical organizations, will outproduce unethical workers in unethical environments any day. Expanding this further and beyond social ethics, a greater sense of cosmic unity, central in Daoist thinking, can provide a sense of relatedness, orderliness, and oneness. This in turn makes business a key factor in sustainability and worldwide integration.

As more and more aspects of production, moreover, are automatized, people increasingly realize that they can live and work creatively rather than for money—fulfilling another Daoist ideal. As Buckminster Fuller says in *Cosmography*, "If humans are not required to earn a living to be provided survival needs, many are going to want very much to be productive, spontaneously taking upon themselves those tasks that society really needs to have done—creatively, productively, and unselfishly." A time is coming when for many people, as Khalil Gibran puts it in *The Prophet*, "work is love made visible."

YouTube: "Little Green Bags: True Business Sustainability"

Read: Egizii, Rita. 2011. "Daoist Principles as a Solution for Sustainable Business." *Journal of Daoist Studies* 4:190-201.

Fuller, Richard Buckminster. 1992. *Cosmography: A Posthumous Scenario for the Future of Humanity*. New York: Macmillan.

Mitroff, Ian I., and Elizabeth A. Denton. 2012. *Spiritual Audit of Corporate America: A Hard Look at Spirituality, Religion, and Values in the Workplace*. San Francisco: Jossey-Bass Publishing.

52. Personal Success

This vision of work as personal fulfillment and a main factor in the creation of social harmony in China today appears in the *Daode jing* reading by Zeng Shijiang 曾仕強 (b. 1934), a certified accountant, historian, and business leader who serves as director of the Yuchai Group. Much of his work focuses on illuminating the successful economic practices and social impact of important historical figures, their "wisdom for life." He has written books on a prime minister of the Zhou dynasty, a leading Tang general, the Ming eunuch Zheng He 鄭和, and the Qing emperor Kangxi. In addition, he also adduces two ancient classics to extol traditional values for the modern age: the *Yijing* and the *Daode jing*.

Regarding the latter, he has two books, *Laozi de rensheng zhihui* 老子的人生智慧 (The Living Wisdom of Laozi) and *Daode jing de aomi* 道德經的奧秘 (The Mystery of the *Daode jing*). The first, also available online as popular lectures in video format, interprets Dao on three levels, as visible and tangible, diffuse and obscure, and ineffable. Applying its wisdom to practical and business life, Zeng recommends flowing smoothly along like water, cultivating the values of being soft and weak, and exercising a form of leadership that provides subtle guidance while encouraging individual skills and initiative.

His second book begins by acknowledging the mysterious nature of the text and emphasizes the degree of disagreement it has engendered over the millennia. It then insists that Laozi and his thought are both "dead and not dead," meaning that they originated many centuries ago and are no longer with us in concrete, physical form. However, they are still alive in spirit, stimulating new ways of thinking that yet recover age-old wisdom. "Even if the age of Laozi is long gone, thousands of years past, his thought and its spirit, that is, the Dao he wanted to convey, is still alive." Borderless and beyond the limitations of any specific culture, this reading open the activation of Laozi's words today.

From here, Zeng focuses on key concepts of Dao, virtue, and naturalness, applying them to the individual person and his or her concrete performance in society. Nonaction, on the other hand, he sees as a more psychological or mental attitude, engendered through the attainment of no desires, unknowing, and intuitive wisdom. Adopting a position of weakness, fluidity, and simplicity by thinking outside the box and applying the dynamics of opposites, one can overcome the strong and rigid, the difficult and even the apparently insurmountable.

To him, studying the *Daode jing* can help people today break through various blind spots in their thinking and open them to the practice of superior wisdom in life, becoming empowered and even invincible. For more detailed practical advice on specific day-to-day situations and issues in the phenomenal world, then, Zeng suggests consulting the *Yijing*, another work about which he has written extensively. Forming a complementary pair with the *Daode jing* in yin-yang fashion, to him it offers practical directives where the text provides an overarching cosmological framework, outlining the "way of heaven" and the key principles to follow in life.

Zeng places strong emphasis on the restoration of Chinese cultural traditions in the modern world and their activation in the actions of each individual. Represented closely by the *Daode jing*, they offer guidelines in the pursuit of material satisfaction and prosperity as well as peace of mind and social stability.

This, moreover, will have a lasting effect on the planet, as the text's focus on the "harmony between humanity and nature" creates a strong ecological awareness that will save the earth in its time of crisis. While many claim that 21st century is the century of science and technology and others call it the digital age, Zeng believes that it is most importantly an era of environmental protection. People need to adopt a more universal perspective and come to see themselves as guests on earth, learning to cherish its resources and love its environment.

YouTube: "The Mystery of Tao Te Ching"

Read: Autry, James A., and Stephen Mitchell. 1998. *Real Power: Business Lessons from the Tao Te Ching*. New York: Riverhead Books.

53. Daoist Psychotherapy

A change in self-perception is also at the center of the *Daode jing* application in cognitive psychotherapy. As described by its founders Albert Ellis and Aaron Beck, it seeks to help the patient overcome difficulties by identifying and changing dysfunctional thinking, behavior, and emotional responses. Identifying distorted thinking, it serves to modify beliefs, behaviors, and relationships. The goal is a greater sense of inner authenticity reached through the appreciation of how one's thoughts and perceptions color emotions and lead to certain kinds of behavior, how certain ways of being in the world are unhelpful and dysfunctional and can be replaced by more appropriate and life-enhancing attitudes.

It is particularly effective in cases of generalized anxiety disorder, a common ailment especially among Chinese and Asian populations. Its key features are excessive worry and anxiety, coupled with overly high expectations of self and others and a general sense of lack of control. It is usually chronic and rather difficult to treat. In its extreme forms it can lead to a decrease in overall functioning, to various physical ailments, and to a shortened life expectancy.

In mainland China, Drs. Zhang Yalin and Yang Desen, based at the Mental Health Institute of Hunan Medical University in Changsha, have utilized the *Daode jing* in this context to create an indigenous form of cognitive therapy. It was introduced into the U.S. under the name Taoist Cognitive Psychotherapy is currently studied in various experiments at the New School for Social Research in New York under the directorship of Doris Chang. It works in three stages of treatment:

1. Orientation and Assessment—developing a therapeutic relationship, introducing the overall principles, pinpointing specific patient problems, and planning the treatment.

2. Doctrine Instruction and Application—teaching key *Daode jing* principles and facilitating their adaptation to specific problems and concerns.

3. Internalization and Reinforcement—summarizing the treatment process, enhancing specific principles, and discussing future application.

The process takes about twelve individual therapy sessions of 45-50 minutes each that occur once or twice a week. Randomized clinical trials in China have shown the effectiveness of the method, not only for generalized anxiety disorder but also for panic attacks and obsessive-compulsive behavior patterns.

Taoist Cognitive Psychotherapy utilizes several sets of principles from the *Daode jing*, beginning with "Benefit without harm to yourself or others; do your best without competing with others" (ch. 81). The *Treatment Manual* personalizes these statements and applies them to the individual in ordinary life. It encourages patients not to take pleasure in the misfortune of others or envy their success. "At the same time, we should not be overly self-critical or self-blaming for our failures, rather strive to do our best within our own capacity." It further notes that strife is often more about internal comparison than outward competition. "Predators will pursue prey in order to survive; they will thus compete with other predators for the same target. However, they do not feel resentment or self-pity that another predator has caught more food" (Chang 2012, 21).

The lesson to be learned is that we should do what we can in life according to our own ability, strive to achieve our own goals while refraining from comparing ourselves with others and seeking their approval. In other words, to live according to the *Daode jing*, we must accurately appraise our capacities, talents, resources, and abilities, adopt a clear view of what we can and should do, then decide how best to act. What is a spiritual statement about the way of heaven and the sage's adaptation to it in the original her is reinterpreted as a way of self-enhancement in Western psychological mode.

The second set of principles has to do with reducing desire, being content with what one has, and knowing when it is enough. The text has, "Moderate desire and limit selfishness; know when it is enough and learn to be content" (chs. 19, 44). To realize this involves a balancing act. On the one hand, "human desires and needs push citizens to progress, resulting in improvements in social and economic development and quality of life driven from self-interest." On the other hand, "excessive personal desire can foster stress, suffering, fatigue, and cause harm to others" (Chang 2012, 25). It is thus important to embrace the virtue of sufficiency and finding contentment.

A third set emphasizes the importance of harmony, modesty, humility, and softness. The original states, "Know harmony and be modest, remember, the soft can overcome the tough (chs. 55, 66), speaking in the context of warfare and political battles rather than personal interactions. In psychotherapy, however, the statements are read to relate to core conflicts within the patient—either external, such as with other people, in the work place, and in terms of social or cultural demand; or internal, referring to issues of pride, shame, self-criticism, perfectionism, and the desire for control.

The fourth and last pair of *Daode jing* principles invokes its key ideals of nonaction and naturalness. "Be clear and still and rest in nonaction; let nature take its course" (chs. 45, 48, 25). Here they indicate "that people should cultivate a state of calm, quiet awareness so that they may see themselves, others, and world *as they are*, not filtered through dysfunctional automatic thoughts or assumptions about how things are." It recommends that patients choose a self-cultivation practice to undertake regularly, "be it meditation or another contemplative practice such as qigong, taichi, yoga, calligraphy, prayer, and the like" (Chang 2012, 33).

Overall, the goal of the therapy, as in the *Daode jing*, is to rest in one's own nature and flow along with the world in a state of nonaction, here understood as "not meddling or interfering with things, letting oneself and the world be: letting oneself be who and what one is, and is on one's way to becoming; letting others be who and what they are, and are on their way to becoming; and letting the world be what it is, and what it is on its way to becoming" (Craig 2007).

YouTube: "Cognitive Behavioral Therapy Simply Explained"

Read: Chang, Doris F. 2012. *Chinese Taoist Cognitive Therapy for Generalized Anxiety Disorder: Treatment Manual*. New York: New School of Social Research.

Craig, Eric. 2007. *Tao Psychotherapy: Introduction a New Approach to Humanistic Practice*. London: Taylor & Francis.

Lu, Xichen. 2011. "Ancient Daoist Philosophy and Authentic Living." In *Living Authentically: Daoist Contributions to Modern Psychology*, edited by Livia Kohn, 25-38. Dunedin, FL: Three Pines Press.

54. Self-Help

A different personal application of *Daode jing* teachings to practical life appears in the teachings of a Buddhist master, the Venerable Konghai 空海. Originally named Guo Yongjin 郭永進, he was born in 1955 in rural Taiwan and felt inspired by Guanyin 观音, the Bodhisattva of Compassion, at an early age. After studying world religions, psychology, and philosophy at the university and completing his military service, he became a doctor of Chinese traditional medicine in 1985. While practicing medicine, he moved on to Buddhist training, studying variously in Taiwan, Thailand, Korea, and Japan. The massive Taiwan earthquake of 1999 pushed him to a new level of enlightenment and, in 2000, he began to teach full-time, soon reaching a high level of popularity throughout the Chinese-speaking world.

His teaching is also increasingly popular in the mainland, available online under the title, "The Wisdom and Application of the *Daode jing*" (*Daode jing de zhihui yu yingyong* 道德經的智慧與應用). It links the worldview of the *Daode jing* with Buddhist concepts of emptiness and practices of meditation. Reading the text chapter by chapter with his followers, he describes Dao as the divine underlying power of all, equal to Buddhist emptiness, Confucian Non-Ultimate, the Christian God, and Muslim Allah.

The root source of all life, Dao supports everyone and everything, making all beings—and especially all people—part of one whole, of one great universal family. Realizing this fundamental oneness, and also the continuity of life and death, people can develop true compassion and live in harmony. They can also connect to inherent wisdom and inner virtue, the pure mind and consciousness at the root of their being, their basic power of intuition and soul potency. Doing so, they overcome knowledge, critical evaluations, as well as religious dogmas and superstitions.

In practical terms, this means, to "make spirit and material souls embrace oneness and not be separate" (ch. 10), here interpreted to let go of all thoughts of past and future—regrets, sins, and inherited karmic patterns as well as the fantasy world of an unreal dreamland—and bring body and heart-and-mind together in the here and now. All thoughts beyond the present lead to nothing but pain and misery, essentially meaningless to living fully and happily. As one is in the present, moreover, one "contains yin and embraces yang" (ch. 42), fully realizing that the mind is part of cosmic emptiness or Dao, while the body is part of the material world—joined together to form the individual.

To reach this level, the main practice is one of "cleansing and purifying the mysterious mirror" (ch. 10), here related to the classical Zen understanding of the mind as a clear mirror, on which no dust should accumulate. The Venerable Konghai distinguishes three types of mirrors.

The most common is bent, concave or convex, twisted and dusty, reflecting the mind's own patterns as determined by bad habits of the ego and negative tendencies, such as arrogance, hatred, and greed. People whose mind is like this always think themselves right and are unable to appreciate another point of view. Without wisdom and compassion, their lives are determined by personal desires and mired in conflict.

The next mirror, less common and achieved through Buddhist study, is partially clear, allowing an opening toward reality and a more open-minded approach to living. Here knowledge is acquired and wisdom awakes. The top level, finally, is the completely clear and bright mirror, a mind that is free from ego-driven desires and reflects reality accurately—resting, in *Daode jing* terms, in a state of perpetual "clarity and stillness" (. 45).

The way to reach this highest level is less one of meditation, still a suspect practice in China, than one of cognitive restructuring, the reorganization of thinking away from egotistical inclinations and toward a more cosmic, universal perspective of Dao. The effect is a great increase in peace of mind and an overarching improvement in the quality of living.

YouTube: "An Introduction on Teachings of Dao De Jing"

Read: https://konghaien.wordpress.com/ven-kong-hai/

55. Individual Realization

Peace of mind and a high quality of living are also the central concern of a growing number of young Chinese, keen to get away from full-time employment, traditional family structures, overarching social requirements, and ever-increasing consumption. Needing little, they typically have some form of gainful employment, yet spend a good portion of their time doing what gives them real satisfaction and engage in philosophical speculation and spiritual practice. While not expressly Daoist, they embody the age-old Daoist ideal of personal cultivation in nonaction and pervasive happiness—personified by the Eight Immortals as much as other reclusive figures.

Many young people pursue their personal realization through travel. They work part of the year, live frugally, often still staying at their parents' house, then take off from their job to venture forth. Some stay in China, hiking around mountains and exploring remote areas, but most go overseas, keeping away from top tourist destinations and crowded cities. Choosing the road less traveled, they find respite and a new openness in far-off corners.

Another model of individual realization is the ideal of the inner-city hermit. One example here is Chen Yuming 陈宇明, an ordained Daoist who rose to vice-abbot of the main monastery on Huashan. Frustrated by bureaucratic procedures, internal bickering, and state interference, he left the mountain and moved to Chengdu, where he lives in a tiny apartment and supports himself by giving calligraphy lessons. Having made his time fully his own, he can practice personal cultivation and truly grow in the Daoism he signed up for to begin with. This, of course, has led to an increase in spiritual prowess, which did not remain hidden. Huang now also travels to run practice workshops, both in China and overseas.

A yet similar case is Chen Kai (CK) as described by Rob Schmitz. Growing up in the small town of Hengyang in Hunan in the 1980s, he would hear his father constantly rant against "the system" that prevented him from pursuing his dreams and stymied his talents. Since his father thought himself a musician, CK too had to play, beginning with the violin and later switching to the accordion. After finishing high school, he went to work for an accordion manufacturer, where his musical and technical expertise catapulted him quickly into a managerial position. Eventually he joined Polvernini, an Italian accordion maker with a branch in Shanghai, and became their man for everything: manager, translator, repair specialist, supply person, customer service agent, and more.

The work was flexible and easy. It provided CK with a good income without taking up too much time. Soon he began to pursue his dream: a sandwich shop along the lines of an American deli. Up on the second floor of a building, with only a small sign to indicate its presence, the shop was rather unsuccessful, although business would pick up every so often. Rob Schmitz describes it as a sanctuary within a sanctuary, a refuge from the pressures of daily life, a peaceful oasis where people could hang out and just be.

Hiring help to do the actual cooking and serving, CK himself would relax, converse with the customers, play his accordion, read spiritual and other literature, and pursue personal self-realization. Engaging in meditation and energy circulation, he became more aware of his internal being, feeling that there was "a real me" inside and having visions of beautiful lands and flowers. Coming to appreciate Buddhist scriptures, he soon learned about a monk outside the city who would provide guidance and teach advanced forms of meditation. This gave his life a yet new and different focus, leading gradually to a greater sense of happiness and, without ever joining a formal religious organization, transformed him into a more spiritual being.

Daoist teachings and practices, in a similar manner, inspire people to live peacefully and frugally, taking up little space and using few resources while pursuing personal cultivation and their own, unique self-realization.

YouTube: "Chinese Millennials Abroad"

Read: Palmer, David A., and Elijah Siegler. 2017. *Dream Trippers: Global Daoism and the Predicament of Modern Spirituality*. Chicago: University of Chicago Press.

Schmitz, Rob. 2016. *Street of Eternal Happiness: Big City Dreams along a Shanghai Road*. New York: Crown Publishers, ch. 1.

56. Chanting

A popular Daoist way of enabling this spiritual transformation is by chanting. Besides the chanting of morning and evening liturgies at Daoist temples, this includes first and foremost the recitation of the *Daode jing* on a regular basis, a bodily technique that also helps to internalize ideas.

The practice goes back to the Han dynasty (206-23 BCE), when students recited the classics to learn them by heart and also as an expression of devotion. The preferred object of recitation at the time was the *Xiaojing* 孝經 (Classic of Filial Piety), not only short and easy to memorize but an inspiration to honor one's elders. In the same way, the *Daode jing*, in the 1st century BCE, especially under the influence of Emperor Jing and his mother, Empress Dou, rose to prominence as a sacred text. It helped people to be more contented with their role, gave them tranquility in their dealings with the world, and increased their understanding of the subtleties of the universe.

In addition to its favorable position at court, the *Daode jing* was also popular among masters of the early sciences (geomancy, medicine, astronomy, fortune-telling) and local officials. They venerated the text and taught it to the people in their communities, causing a gradual maturation of its ideas in the popular mind. Soon recitation became part of established culture. Philosophers of the Later Han recited it continuously, so they would behave calmly and in a socially conscientious manner. Several well-situated men even took it as a guide and distributed their fortunes among the poor.

Once popular Daoist cults appeared on the scene, the text became a scared scripture, representing the revealed emanation of pure Dao. Not only a guide to personal and political conduct, it became a source of magical efficacy, whose frequent recitation could bring good fortune, exorcise demons, and cure diseases.

This tradition continues today. Daoist masters encourage regular recitation of the *Daode jing* to create merit and deepen understanding. The practice also enhances personal cultivation, fostering an inner alignment with key teachings of the religion and the energies of Dao. They teach it both in public classes, as those held on Saturday afternoons at Chengdu's Qingyang gong (Black Sheep Temple), and privately to select disciples. The ideal practice is to chant the whole text daily, either in one sitting—which takes about an hour—or divided into two, practicing morning and evening. After doing this for some time, adepts copy it by hand, to eventually memorize it by heart. It has a transformative effect. As Ian Johnson notes, after experiencing even one chanting session, "The world outside felt far away, and the text felt present in our bodies."

Reaching beyond the immediate religious environment, some educators such as Master Nan, a reclusive intellectual living near Lake Tai, claim that the *Daode jing* can help students both through its content and its very words. They suggest that the systematic, repeated recitation of the text, as "their brains are hardwired by the beauty of Laozi's language, helps children concentrate better, reduce anxiety, eliminate bad habits, improve social awareness, and generally lay a good foundation for life." Self-help gurus, moreover, recommend regular chanting, ideally helped online with relaxing music, birdsong, and pictures of flowers, to lower blood pressure and improve metabolic function, releasing panic reactions and help people attain their optimal weight.

YouTube: "Tanwen (Daoist Chanting)"

"Wuji (Daoist Chanting)"

Read: Kohn, Livia. 1998. "The *Tao-te-ching* in Ritual." In *Lao-tzu and the Tao-te-ching*, edited by Livia Kohn and Michael LaFargue, 143-61. Albany: State University of New York Press.

Johnson, Ian. 2017. *The Souls of China: The Return of Religion after Mao*. New York: Pantheon Books.

57. Internal Alchemy

Reaching beyond these practical goals and elementary recitation, some practitioners hope to develop fully into spiritual beings by training in the dominant form of Daoist meditation, known as internal alchemy (*neidan* 内丹). Prevalent since the Song dynasty, it combines concepts of operative alchemy and cosmological speculation with the visualization of body energies. Its goal is the systematic transformation of sexual essence (*jing* 精) first into vital energy (*qi* 气), then into spirit (*shen* 神), and eventually into oneness with Dao, actively reversing human gestation and cosmic creation.

Adepts begin by focusing on essence, the tangible form of *qi* that rests in the abdomen in men and the chest in women, manifesting as semen and menstrual blood respectively. To revert this to *qi*, men allow a feeling of arousal to occur, then guide the flowing energy back up along the spine and into the head, thus "subduing the white tiger." Women, when they feel menstrual energy sink down, massage their breasts and visualize it rising upward to transform back from blood into *qi*. Over several months, this will cause menstruation to cease, the "decapitation of the red dragon."

Both then circulate the newly purified *qi* in the microcosmic orbit, guiding it along the central channels up the spine and down the front of the torso, opening a series of passes or barriers along the way. Not only strengthening the body and enhancing health, this *qi*-circulation eventually leads to the manifestation of a concentrated pearl of primordial *qi*—newly formed in men, present from birth in women. The first stage concludes when the pearl coalesces.

The second stage is the same for men and women. It focuses on the transformation of purified *qi* into spirit. Practitioners identify yin and yang as different energies in the body, each described with different metaphors depending on the level of purity attained. They include yang symbolized by heart, fire, lead, dragon, and the red bird; and yin represented by the kidneys, water, mercury, tiger, and the white tiger. At each stage of the transmutation process, the energies are given different names and metaphors. Eventually adepts learn not only to mix them in the abdomen but to revolve them through an inner-body cycle and refine them to a celestial level of purity. Spirit emerges as an independent entity, and the pearl gives rise to the immortal embryo.

Once the embryo starts to grow, adepts switch their practice to nourish it with embryo respiration, which also makes them increasingly independent of outer nourishment and air. While the first phase was easier for men, this stage is easier for women, because they are naturally endowed with the faculty to grow an embryo. After ten months, the embryo is complete.

Adepts then proceed to the third stage. They transform the as yet semi-material body of the embryo into the pure spirit body of the immortals, a body of primordial *qi*. After nourishing it to completion, they allow it to take birth by moving it up along the spine and letting it exit through the top of the head, reaching celestial rebirth. After passing into the heavenly spheres, the spirit communicates with the gods and fully transcends the limitations of the body.

After this birth, adepts continue to nurse it for three years, during which it moves faster and travels ever farther. As the spirit enters into its cosmic ventures, adepts exhibit enhanced faculties and gain powers of direct interaction with the gods. These powers are also essential for the successful performance of Daoist ritual, so that not only meditators but also ritual practitioners require thorough training in the procedures of internal alchemy.

YouTube: "Guided Microcosmic Orbit Meditation"

Read: Kohn, Livia, and Robin R. Wang, eds. 2009. *Internal Alchemy: Self, Society, and the Quest for Immortality*. Magdalena, NM: Three Pines Press.

Wilhelm, Richard. 1962 [1929]. *The Secret of the Golden Flower*. New York: Harcourt, Brace and World.

58. Wang Liping

The most prominent teacher of Daoist internal alchemy in China today is Wang Liping 王力平. As outlined in his biography, translated by Thomas Cleary (1997), he was originally called Wang Yongsheng 王永生 and later obtained the Daoist name Linglingzi 灵灵子 (Master of the Numinous). He was born June 6, 1949 in Fushun 抚顺 near Changbaishan 长白山 in the far northeastern province of Liaoning, as the second son of a working-class family. In 1960, when he was eleven years old, three Daoist masters, representatives of the Dragon Gate lineage of Laoshan in Shandong, after exhaustive prognostication, sought him out to become their successor. They included a martial arts master, a senior physician, and a top-level acupuncturist.

They tutored Wang over a sixteen-year period, which can be divided into three major phases. During the first, 1960-1966, they stayed near his home, so that he could continue to go to school. They trained him in the fundamentals, strengthening his body and mind with various forms of martial arts as well as standing and sitting meditations. The second phase, 1966-1970, saw the brunt of the Cultural Revolution. Fleeing from the Red Guards, Wang and his masters took to the hills and stayed hidden, wandering all over the country. At this point, he learned the cultivation process of internal alchemy.

During the third phase, 1970-1976, with revolutionary fervor abating, they continued wandering, but spent time on major Daoist mountains, including Huashan and Louguantai, to practice in caves and connect to other Daoists. The masters instructed him in the advanced skills of supplementary Daoist techniques, including fengshui, fortune-telling, prognostication, medicine, and acupuncture.

After the end of the Cultural Revolution, they all went home. The three masters retreated back to Laoshan to restore what they could. Wang Liping, following their guidance, returned to his family who were dirt-poor but had survived intact. He took a job in a factory, got married, had a son, and to all intents and purposes led an ordinary life. A decade later, in 1985, the masters decreed that he should emerge from concealment, and he began to give lectures and workshops. Like many other spiritual leaders in Asia, the Daoists had decided that the late 20th century was the time when the various esoteric teachings and subtle practices of their tradition should spread and become available to spiritual seekers among the general populace. Wang Liping became their major spokesperson.

His first venture was a one-month workshop near Beijing, with about a hundred participants that focused on breathing, energy circulation, quiet sitting, personal healing, and fundamental Daoist thought. Following this, while still working a regular job, he would travel to cities all over the country to teach. Gradually followers became more sincere, participation in his workshops increased, his lectures and demonstrations drew tens of thousands, and prominent popular and political figures came to learn from him.

All this came to a crushing end with the Falungong crack-down in 1999. Wang moved back into shadows and only emerged again in 2007, when he offered his first public lectures and taught a group of Europeans. Since then, however, his following has grown substantially, he teaches actively both in China and overseas, and many travel to his center in Dalian for in-depth instruction and training.

YouTube: "Opening the Dragon Gate—Taoist Wizard"

Read: Cleary, Thomas. 1997. *Opening the Dragon Gate: The Making of a Modern Taoist Wizard*. By Chen Kaiguo and Zheng Shunchao. Tokyo: Tuttle.

59. Practice Groups

Wang Liping's teaching has spread far and wide, and there are a number of practice groups in China itself. Ian Johnson describes one in Beijing, led by Qin Ling, the wife of Xiao Weijia, who in turn is the son of a well-known Party poet and propagandist. Inheriting his father's apartment, he still lives in the cadre complex west of Tian'anmen Square, an area for the longest time off limits to foreigners but now quite easily accessible.

Here Qin Ling assembles her students for the practice of internal alchemy. A small group, they follow the outline of the alchemical process in the *Lingbao bifa* 灵宝毕法 (Secret Methods of Numinous Treasure) and *Taiyi jinhua zongzhi* 太乙金华宗旨 (The Secret of the Golden Flower), manuals from the 12th and 16th centuries, together with works by Wang Liping himself. Their practice focuses on fundamentals, notably breathing, walking, and quiet sitting.

Breathing involves deep, rhythmic inhalations and exhalations that expand and contract the diaphragm. The posture—always centrally important—is sitting cross-legged with straight back, lips lightly closed, the tongue on top of the palate (to connect the central energy channels in the torso), head upright, and eyes lightly closed.

Letting thoughts come and go, the idea is to allow the bright light of cosmic spirit to manifest on the far horizon, then pull it toward the body, enter it through the third eye, and spread it all over. An intensification occurs when breathing is reversed, that is, when the abdomen and lungs are intentionally contracted upon inhalation and expanded during exhalation, increasing control over the *qi* in the body.

Walking means focused breathing during movement: inhale and exhale once every six paces; alternatively, inhale for three, hold the breath for three, exhale for three, and hold again for three. Practitioners should keep their heads up, chests out, and arms moving back and forth, "like a leader inspecting the troops." Done quite fast and for up to an hour without stopping, it increases depth of breath, intensity of movement, and overall physical stamina.

Quiet sitting is the classic form of Daoist meditation. It usually begins with concentration on the breath to calm the mind. Then, in its alchemical mode, it involves the visualization and spreading of divine light through the body, circulating it through the organs for purification, then settling it in the lower elixir field where eventually the immortal embryo will grow. The practice involves sitting motionless for several hours (ideally in full lotus), which is excruciating in the beginning and only gets less painful over years of practice.

Meditation and breathing are also the focus of formal one-week or ten-day retreats, some of which draw as many as 500 people. They come from all walks of life, including lawyers, businessmen, musicians, painters, filmmakers, and more. Supported by Party officials who emphasize their importance in developing the new "harmonious society" and enhance "traditional culture"—current Party speak for "religion"—the retreats take place in rebuilt temples and involve chanting of hymns, listening to lectures—typically rather confusing—as well as focused Daoist practice. Besides blessings of a great Daoist master, participants take away a quieter mind, a deeper sense of self, and a greater awareness of cosmic connection. At the same time, they support the growth of Daoism in China today.

These features are also what attracts a growing number of Westerners to Wang's Daoism. Thus, in September 2008, a group of eight Romanian seekers joined him at his center in Dalian, quickly reaching higher levels of internal cultivation and signing up as formal disciples. Joining him once a year, they travel to China and also organize retreats in Europe, typically assembling fifty-some participants for intensive practice. In the U. S., groups have developed in various parts of the country under the banner of Dragongate Academy, similarly visiting China and/or holding sessions closer to home.

Check: "Taoist Master Wang Liping 2012"

Read: Johnson, Ian. 2017. *The Souls of China: The Return of Religion after Mao*. New York: Pantheon Books.

Toader, Serban. 2018. "A Romanian Spiritual Seeker's Growth: From SciFi Readings to Neidan." *Journal of Daoist Studies* 11.

60. The Future

Given increasing globalization and the shrinking of time and space—through instant communication and ever faster travel—the political, economic, and cultural developments I have described in these pages are set on a course of continuous increase and intensification.

China, faced with numerous issues in all three areas, has a number of options. As David Shambaugh points out, there are four models of governance it can follow. Radical totalitarianism as under Mao or complete democratization as in Taiwan are the more extreme and much less likely options. More probable is a form of authoritarianism, either hard as today or soft as in the early 2000s. Most likely is an alternation between the two, depending on the leader's personality at the top and the degree of economic and social tension at the bottom.

The majority of the Chinese people are excessively tired of being pushed around by Party campaigns and have never even thought about free elections. They accept one-party rule and official corruption as a given but want more say in issues that concern them directly. These include most importantly the social network—unemployment, social security, health care, and education—and to a lesser degree legal issues, such as household registration, ownership of real estate, business rights, and intellectual property. In addition, as more people rise into the middle class, they begin to use their disposable income for personal improvement through better food, wider travel, increased learning, health improvement, and self-cultivation.

It is in these areas that Daoism has its main impact and is actively creating models and inspiration, from community-building temples and eco-friendly resorts through holistic clinics and organic food to exercise, self-help, chanting, and meditation. Rooted deeply in traditional Chinese culture, Daoism has yet a highly modern and alternative aura, making it attractive to people of many different walks of life. This holds true for China as much as the West, where large segments of the population have been engaged in self-cultivation and personal life-improvement for several decades and where Chinese medicine, forms of exercise, and Daoist wisdom already have a firm place.

Both in East and West, Daoism plays an important role in empowering the individual. It categorically states, as Roger Ames says, that "we are all capable of repudiating the distorting influences of civilization and recovering our original nature," creating the life we want and are best suited for, while supporting people, life, and nature around us. According to Daoism, each individual has the power to limit procreation, reduce accumulation, refrain from exercising power, and refuse to give in to economic, political, and social pressure. Daoists assert that anyone can practice peaceful coexistence, cultivate himself to perfect health, eat a simple and nutritious diet, and live in sufficiency, peace, and moral integrity, spending his or her free time leisurely in cultural and spiritual pursuits. Dedicating themselves to Dao, moreover, human beings can create communities that embrace these values and develop a form of life on earth that is as close to perfection as imaginable at this level in human development.

YouTube: "China's Future Megaprojects"

Read: Ames, Roger T. 1994. *The Art of Rulership: A Study of Ancient Chinese Political Thought*. Honolulu: University of Hawaii Press.

Shambaugh, David. 2016. *China's Future*. Cambridge: Polity Press.

Index